SCIENTIFIC MANAGEMENT IN RUSSIA:

WORLD-CLASS SCHOOLS AND SCHOLARS

By

GRIGORIY Z. SHCHERBAKOVSKIY

Book 1.   A.K. Gastev and TsIT

Science editor and author of preface: Prof. E.B. Koritskiy, Doctor of Economics

ISBN: 978-0-692-31405-0

NEW YORK, NEW YORK
2014

TABLE OF CONTENTS

Preface by science editor

Once I was introduced to Prof. Shcherbakovskiy's project "Scientific Management in Russia: World-class Schools and Scholars" I agreed to join it as the science editor right away.

This project will make an exciting contribution to historical studies. It will include four books on four prominent pioneers of scientific management in Russia: A.K. Gastev, N.A. Vitke, F.R. Dunaevsky and A.A. Bogdanov.

Some might wonder whether it makes sense to reproduce and analyze ideas and concepts that are a century old. Since I strongly believe in the importance and value of historical studies on any science, particularly scientific management, I would see no need in making my case. However, many authors trust that "any modern student knows more than any scholar in the pertinent field a hundred years ago." For instance, A. Pigou, a leading economist in his time, turned down an offer to review a study on the *Theories of Value before Adam Smith* as follows: "These antiquarian researches have no great attraction for one who finds it difficult enough to read what now is though on economic problems, without spending time in studying confessedly inadequate solutions that were offered centuries ago."[1] Henry Ford, a trailblazer for scientific management

---

[1] Quoted from: Blaug M. Economic Theory in Retrospect, Cambridge, 1985. P.1.

and the founder of an economic miracle such as the Ford Motor Company, was even more straightforward. Proud of his own truly outstanding achievements,[2] he openly scorned history as "more or less bunk" and believed the history that matters is what we make today. Well, by the same token there would be little need in studying Ford's own works, as "any business school student" indeed knows much more than the father of the automobile industry who put America on wheels and changed it – as well as the entire planet – forever.

With all due respect to Pigou and Ford, to their work and accomplishments, I cannot share their arrogance towards their predecessors. This *radical absolutist* approach essentially denies history the right to exist, since it is deemed to be "more or less bunk". Some *moderate absolutists* do not reject the historical approach at large but believe that older works must be assessed against current theoretical criteria. This is why absolutists often see little value in historical studies and even get exasperated with the lack of today's terminology and notations. This is why they look down on early ideas and concepts, calling them "mistakes", "fallacies", "wrong opinions of dead men" and so on and so forth. Such opinions tend to ignore certain intrinsic factors such as the paucity of analytical methods faced by early authors or their social, economic, political and ideological environment. Absolutism in history, therefore, suggests that the modern reader should – at best – be informed only about those pioneers of Russian management whose ideas still hold and, moreover, meet the stringent criteria of today's science, while other authors of the past should be simply forgotten.

The *relativist* approach to history of knowledge is entirely different. Old theories, according to this philosophy, should be evaluated in terms of their own standards and analyzed in an empathic and benevolent way in the context of their epoch. However, relativists are also facing a considerable risk, albeit of a different nature, that of glorifying early authors and exaggerating

---

[2] Ford H. My Life and Work. Garden City, NY, 1922.

the significance of their findings (regrettably, the author of this preface occasionally succumbed to this temptation as well). The most appropriate attitude, therefore, should probably synthesize these two approaches without their excesses. This is exactly what Professor Shcherbakovskiy's project is all about. Its success is for the reader to judge; as for myself, I'm highly optimistic and will tell more about it in due course. Let me just note now that a balanced discussion of ideas and concepts of the best Russian scientific management scholars along with the publication of their selected works certainly seems to be a relevant and fair initiative.

Indeed, retrospective studies are critical to a discipline such as management where the entire "contemporary theory wears the scars of yesterday's problems."[3] W. Duncan suggests that lessons from the classical heritage must be learned by all managers because history is not a reminder "of our follies and crimes" but rather *"an encouraging remembrance of generative souls"*. Getting to know what these persons wrote is "the most efficient start for studies in the science of management. This is why such heritage is so valuable."[4] We can also talk about the direct benefits of this knowledge. It often helps avoid mistakes made in the past; some forgotten solutions found in old days may turn out to be of use today. Duncan says that "management history is full of valuable lessons for those who attend to what it can teach."[5]

However, there is more to history than "valuable lessons". The interest in works by Russian pioneers of scientific management includes something larger than "pragmatic benefits" and less simple than "love for the old times". Indeed, each new generation of scholars has a moral duty to study their predecessors' heritage.

---

[3] Blaug M. Economic Theory in Retrospect, Cambridge, 1985. P. XXIV.
[4] Duncan W. J. Great Ideas in Management. Jossey-Bass Publishers. San Francisco-Oxford, 1990. P.9
[5] Ibid. P.11

Without fearing the lofty style, to know the history of management thought and its precious legacy, as well as to master classic methodologies is critical to any breakthrough in academic research.

Where does the history of scientific management start is another matter. For instance, construction managers of Egyptian pyramids certainly had brilliant organizational skills and excellent experience. Some authors argue that historical studies into management should begin with the Old Testament, a treasure trove of wisdom. No doubt that Moses, Isaiah and other patriarchs and prophets offer a wealth of knowledge. On the other hand, is it worth to go to ancient history and times immemorial? I do not think so. Management as a *discipline* did not emerge when people started to "manage". Rather, it appeared with the start of *scientific research* to produce systematic theories and develop principles and recommendations to improve management practices.[6]

Curiously enough, scientific management, in contrast to the vast majority of disciplines, has a date of birth universally recognized by the academic community. This relatively young science celebrated its centennial just a quarter of a century ago, in 1986. It is believed to be born in 1886 at the meeting of the American Society of Mechanical Engineers where Henry Towne delivered an address titled "The Engineer as an Economist." Duncan notes that this paper was not overly deep; the author merely called upon engineers to be interested in more than the *technological efficiency,* to be able to calculate costs, revenue and profit, i.e. master the elements of *economic* management. The meeting, however, was attended by an engineer whose ideas soon laid the cornerstone of a new science. That was Frederick Taylor, who went down in history as "the father of scientific management."[7] His works dating back to the late 19th and early 20th century, along with those by other American scholars such as the F. and L. Gilbreth

---

[6] Ibid. P 15.
[7] Ibid. P. 13.

couple, H. Gantt and H. Ford, *initiated scientific management and set global standards for this discipline.*

Despite the resistance and sweeping attacks on the new science from conservatives adhering to routine or "traditional" methods of management, the influence of ideas suggested by Taylor and his fellow scholars was growing rapidly in the USA as well as internationally. Henry Louis le Chate and Lyndall Urwick promoted these ideas in France and Great Britain respectively. Scientific management soon became renowned in Germany, Denmark, Holland and elsewhere in Europe, as well as in Japan (since 1912). In other words, Taylorism spread to all industrialized countries. Prominent scholars who emerged in Europe to formulate new original world-class concepts included, first and foremost, H. Fayol (France), L. Urwick (Great Britain) and E. Schmalenbach (Germany).

Let us now turn to the history of scientific management in Russia where it was known for many years under the name of NOT (the abbreviation of Russian "scientific organization of labor").

It would be wrong to assume that scientific management was non-existent in Russia before 1920s. According to A.K. Gastev, its advent dates back to the same period as in the USA and Europe. As early as in 1904 "somewhere in the Urals, in Lysva and elsewhere attempts were made to apply NOT principles."[8] It appears we should assume the birth of scientific management in Russia dates back to this time. Note, however, that such attempts were spontaneous rather than systematic and at that point had no relation to Taylorism yet. We also hardly know anything about their quality. Classical Taylorism started penetrating Russia somewhat later, in 1908-1909, to experience a true boom in 1911-1914. Taylor's ideas were vividly discussed by students, professors,

---

[8] The Beginning of NOT. Forgotten Discussions and Ideas that Never Came to Life. [*U istokov NOT: Zabytye diskussii i nerealizovannye idei*] / Ed. by E.B. Koritskiy. Leningrad, 1990, P. 50-51.

theory, and F. Herzberg developed his theory of motivation. During these three decades the West laid the groundwork for the buoyant development of qualitative and systems approaches as well as many other theories. Unfortunately, Russian scientific management scholars were then isolated from these new trends by the iron curtain.

The reasons for this tragic decline in Russian scientific management can hardly be separated from the general changes in the USSR after the New Economic Policy was discontinued. The transition from the market economy to Stalin's administrative command system in the late 1920s and early 1930s essentially legitimized subjectivism and arbitrary rule in the economy. Scientific management was increasingly referred to as "a bourgeois fabrication." Virtually all world-renowned NOT institutes and laboratories were closed down, creative discussions on management problems stopped, innovation and research departments at ministries and enterprises were liquidated, including the Workers' and Peasants' Inspectorate (RKI) itself. The government now wanted to rely upon a "strong" executive who would have a monopoly on management in his area and diligently if not blindly follow directives from the Center.

Happily, by the end of the 1950s and the beginning of the 1960s scientific management in Russia finally started recovering from this major crisis. First of all, the political atmosphere changed as the period of brutal Stalinist repressions gave way to Khruschev's "thaw" that generally was conducive to scientific research and discussions. "The thaw" provided access to Western management literature and a greater intellectual freedom. Moreover, industrial growth and the increasing number of economic links called for more sophisticated management systems. Another reason was the impact of new technologies that helped address management problems. All these factors gave rise to the rebirth of scientific management in Russia. However, we were still way behind the Western science, and this gap was getting wider with the passage of time. Indeed, until the early 1990s Russian scientific management had to deal with the *socialist* economic system and its limitations. Even the word "management" in Russian literature was an inevitably pejorative term that applied only to Western science. It was not before the events in August 1991 that this term gained legitimate currency. Countless "business and management schools", courses and seminars, consultancies large and small sprung up. The new generation was free of old ideological prejudices and could think in an uninhibited and independent way. Hundreds of universities established management chairs or departments. Textbooks and monographs, mostly in translation, were printed in millions of copies. One may say that with the liquidation of fundamental socialist values the Russian management theory finally got a chance to "catch up" with the West and join the global mainstream. However, Russia still has a long way to go before it reaches the world level in this field.

Therefore I have to emphasize once again that *truly world level scholars* who enjoyed international recognition and founded strong schools existed in Russia only in 1920s, during the impressive period of assertion and rapid development of scientific management in the country.

Regretfully, modern Western management historians often keep silence about this fact and pay little tribute to Russian scholars. Take, for instance, John Shelldrake; in his "Management Theory: From Taylorism to Japanization" (International Thomson Business Press, 1996) he considers the teachings of 20 major scholars who determined the progress and evolution in this area from its inception in the end of the XIX century till the 80s and 90s of the XX century. No doubt all these scholars played a key role in the history of scientific management, though the eminent historian did "hurt" some outstanding Western scientists such as P. Drucker of R. Ackoff who are conspicuously absent from his monograph.

11

thoroughly reviewed, and some ideas just outlined in earlier papers have been developed further.

In conclusion I would like to thank all our colleagues at St. Petersburg University of Economics and Finance who read the manuscript of this first book of the project and made constructive suggestions. My special gratitude goes to Prof. G.V.Nintsieva who kindly agreed to write one of the books for this project.

I am also indebted to Prof. E.B. Koritskiy, the project science editor, for his helpful advice, "tips" and, in many cases, the final wording.

PART 1. Gastev's system: theoretical ideas, training and practical innovation.

Current publications on the inception and evolution of scientific management, as well as management textbooks pay well-deserved tribute to early management systems developed by Taylor, Gantt, Ford, Fayol and other authors regarded as classics. Unfortunately, little attention is paid to the works of A.K. Gastev, an outstanding Russian scholar, whose system can and must rank among those mentioned above.

Biographical note. Aleksey Kapitonovich Gastev was a well-known economist, sociologist, author and poet. He was born on September 26, 1882 in Suzdal to a teacher's family. After vocational training Gastev enrolled in a teaching college only to be expelled later for political activism that he was involved in since adolescence. In 1901 Gastev joined the Russian Social Democratic Workers' Party. As an avid revolutionary he was arrested, jailed and banished several times. In 1907 he left the Bolshevik Party on ideological grounds.

Gastev had an ample industrial and managerial experience. Before the revolution he was employed for many years as a metal worker in Russia and France (where he graduated from the School for Advanced Studies in Social Sciences). After the October revolution he held executive positions at factories in Moscow, Kharkov and Gorky. He also worked as the secretary of the Metal Workers' Trade Union and held other ranking posts; in particular, Gastev was one of the Proletarian Culture Association (Proletkult) leading ideologists.

In his poems, short stories and essays Gastev celebrated industrialism and looked forward to a new era of humans who would be continuously putting their everyday life in perfect order.

TsIT's development strategy was based on Gastev's brilliant idea that scientific management scholars were to be active in three fundamental areas, i.e. theoretical research, consultations and practical innovation, as well as training and continuous education for skilled workmen and managers.

Professor Monroi from Germany noted in TsIT's guestbook that "Such a combination of a *research* and *educational* institution as yet does not exist in Western Europe."[16] We can echo this prominent scholar by saying that **Gastev formulated and implemented one of the most valuable ideas in the world history of scientific management, namely the concept of its "triune" development.** Life has shown this three-prong approach to be a solid foundation for the progress of scientific management. As G.Kh. Popov, a renowned author, put it a quarter of a century ago, "whenever one of these three components is partially or completely ignored, chances for the emergence and elaboration of a management theory would be much slimmer if exist at all."[17] The "triune" approach has clearly become central to the successful operation of modern American and European academic centers, business schools and management consultancies.

TsIT's structure was adopted to pursuing each of the three components of this mechanism. Its research facilities included a photo and film laboratory that recorded workers' motions; a technological laboratory to improve and develop work implements; biomechanical, physiotechnological and psychotechnical laboratories that studied labor motions, energy metabolism, fatigue and work speed; an educational laboratory to develop fast and efficient training methods for workers and administrators; a social engineering laboratory that focused on individual industrial

---

[16] Glushkov V.M., Dobrov G.M., Tereshchenko V.I. Conversations about management. *[Besedy ob upravlenii].* MOSCOW, 1974. P. 191.
[17] Popov G.Kh. Management theory issues. *[Problemy teorii upravleniya].* Moscow, 1974. P. 256-257.

operations as well as management processes. The social engineering lab became the heart of the TsIT Consultation Department that organized pilot stations and management stations to deal with practical improvements at various institutions and enterprises (for more details see appropriate chapters below).

As for the education function, TsIT was concurrently running several courses, including those for "shop floor instructors", "industrial administrators" and "industrial accountants."[18]

This is how the first and largest scientific management research facility in the country was established and launched. There is no need to dwell on the financial problems faced by TsIT, especially at its early stages, when the Institute had "zero" equipment and "getting every single key and every single desk meant red tape and hassle."[19] Let us continue with theoretical concepts put forward by Gastev and his school.

2. New setups in culture and labor

Though Gastev quit the Bolshevik party, he welcomed the October revolution with a measure of enthusiasm as an outburst of "fresh barbarism" and "a proud rebellion". His publications encouraged the reader "to accept all this without reservations as an emotional and political manifesto of our times". He claimed that one should "surrender to the vortex of the new era where brave rationalism should prevail."[20] These were not empty words: Gastev himself was a model of diligent work and "brave rationalism" as the founder of TsIT.

---

[18] "Vremya", 1923, No.1. P. 69.
[19] Management and research at the Institute of Labor. *[Organizatsionnaya i nauchnaya zhizn Instituta truda].* "Organizatsiya truda", 1921, No.1. P. 120.
[20] Gastev A.K. Our objectives. [Nashi zadachi] / The Beginning of NOT. Forgotten Discussions and Ideas that Never Came to Life. [*U istokov NOT: Zabytye diskussii i nerealizovannye idei*]. Leningrad, 1990, P. 33.

Nevertheless, while "surrendering to the vortex of the new era", Gastev did make some reservations and, in contrast to many researchers, paid due regard to the horrendous side of the revolution. "Too much has been destroyed, - he wrote, - destruction bordering on insanity is effacing chronology…" Chanting *La Marseillaise* and waving red flags came hand-in-hand with "a true black banner of dirt, soot, civil war, famine and cannibalism." Countless generations were spending their best efforts for centuries to create one of the greatest countries in the world. This country was now hopelessly drawn into an abyss, destroying entire industries to bury them under its debris. The national economy suffered a major disaster reminding the darkest periods in European history."

Culture suffered an equally fatal blow. Gastev wrote that the revolution had experimentally and "with an almost laboratory precision proven that grassroots upheavals and grassroots reactions at our times come at a price of a *cultural catastrophe.*"[21]

The revolution presumably started an era of creation and reconstruction of the economy that had been all but destroyed by that same revolution, civil war and the policy of "war communism". Yet almost all population groups, including revolutionaries and counterrevolutionaries, priests and atheists, youths and old men, workers and capitalists, seemed to be infected with a lack of faith, skepticism and apathy. While the times called for initiative, resourcefulness and good governance, millions of educated and intelligent people were suffering a lethargic delusion that "the West will help us somehow".

Gastev firmly believed that economic resurrection in Russia was not feasible without a radical cultural change that should start with addressing the "elementary lack of discipline" and "lax attitude to work and everyday life." Russians in the capital, in towns and villages could call this a trivial matter because they spend their time

---

[21] Gastev A.K. The revolt of culture. *[Vosstanie kultury]*. Kharkov, 1923. P. 13.

pondering on global issues and have no idea that in Europe and the USA a multimillion army of bureaucrats works like a clock, while thousands-strong armies of workers and administrators come to the factory and leave it within a period of five minutes.

"It's indeed time to wake up! It's high time to establish cultural brigades from those few who accept the new speed of life, the new precision of its steps, the uncluttered lines of progress that can transform time into space and space into time."[22] A new movement must be established whose main motto would be civilized and "inexorably steady". We should also rely upon new managers who would "hate the anemic speculation of home-grown schemes and love the practical flexibility bordering on innovation."[23]

Therefore, Gastev believed that a successful social and economic recovery in Russia requires a fundamentally new life and work culture that would rule out apathy, skepticism and lack of faith. *New cultural setups are needed to wake people up from lethargy and inspire them with energy and enthusiasm.*

What was Gastev's idea of these new cultural setups? They were such "biological and social qualities that guarantee a cultural and social victory to their bearer. A social victory here is a broad term that includes, first and foremost, a victory at the economic front."[24]

A schematic of the forthcoming new culture according to Gastev consists of seven basic elements such as:

1. *Acute power of observation.*

---

22 Ibid. P. 7.
23 Ibid. P. 9.
24 Gastev A.K. The new cultural setup. *[Novaya kulturnaya ustanovka".* Moscow, 1923. P. 14.

Gastev thought it to be the very first quality to be nurtured. Russians who tend to be "somewhat dreamy, impulsive and generous" need to be taught good observation skills, an ability to "clearly distinguish between different phenomena" and, last but not least, a capacity for "recording observations with microscopic precision." The notorious "patriotic clumsiness" that is so typical of Russian mentality and runs through all our fairy tales, jokes and fiction "must be completely eradicated." According to Gastev, the power of observation should be taught from early childhood to all schoolchildren, young workers, all workers and peasants, or, in other words, to all citizens.[25]

2. *Care for tools*

Any tool, Gastev wrote, be it an industrial cutter bit, a drill, an axe or hammer, must be appreciated as a treasure. Even if the near future belongs to sophisticated machines and instruments, people should learn to love even the most primitive tools. In fact, "a whole cult of tools should be established as well as a new serious science concerning the laws of their use."

3.   *Biomechanics of labor*

Rapid global industrialization is a major feature of our times when "everything develops under the sign of machinery." The human body – especially in Russia – has "a pathetic destiny" in this environment. Only doctors care for the body – and they do so just because it is their official duty. Gastev implores "to look at man from a new perspective" in the context of the new industrial philosophy and realize that the human being is "one of the most perfect machines ever known to our engineers."[26] A crucial task is

---

[25] Gastev A.K. The revolt of culture. P. 13-14, 22.
[26] Ibid. P. 22.

to "study this magnificent machine, that is, the human body. This machine features a luxury of automatic reactions and can be launched fast... It has a motor, a "transmission", shock absorbers, advanced brakes, delicate regulators and even pressure gauges. All this needs to be studied and used. A special discipline of biomechanics..."[27] should study the capabilities of the human body as a machine aware of its statics and kinematics that "continuously produces new combinations of motions."

4.   The art of energy-efficient labor

Profuse sweating during work often shows a lack of *work culture* rather than the difficulty of the job. "We distribute our efforts as true barbarians... and, however strange it may sound, we do not know how to relax properly." Gastev thought that human energy metabolism must be urgently investigated. He complained that mountains of books were published on thermal energy, on furnaces, boilers, steam engines, electricity and the like, while nothing had been written about the energy of a worker. Not a single line tells us how live human energy should be obtained and consumed!

In the age of chronographs that are accurate to within a ten thousandth of a second, in the age of current and voltage meters, we should learn to measure human energy as well. Human nutrition must become a science similar to those dealing with the feeding of a steam engine or an electric motor; human energy consumption should be measured to a thousandth of a calorie, and control over the operation of human body should be seen in terms of a system of carburetors that supply energy to thermal machines. "We need a radical revolution in this area."[28]

---

[27] Ibid. P. 14-15.
[28] Ibid. P. 15, 23.

5.   Selection of personal types

The new cultural setups imply that workers should be selected according to their psychological profile, and their characters should be "sorted". "Our epoch is critical, - wrote Gastev, - it is a daring time that calls for faith, severity, courage and tight nerves... this epoch requires a careful selection of workers. It would be inexcusable to hire a person as an executive just because he is a professor or just because he calls himself a Communist. Such people must be subject to at least half a year of internship when they would be carefully observed and their psychological reactions would be measured and recorded. A character reference should be issued after such internship."[29]

6.   Training

This area, according to Gastev, is "a true virgin land never trodden by theoreticians or practitioners". A labor training science is therefore urgently needed. "Violinists, dancers, acrobats and fencers are all appropriately trained, yet no proper training exists in the most important area of work skills." Special methodologies should be developed to teach millions of workers "how to deal the right blow, to put the right pressure and distribute stress". A new discipline, the pedagogy of labor, would move labor culture away from the "dead point". It might be desirable to start labor training much earlier than at 14 or 16 (as permitted by labor laws), maybe even at the age of 2, "at least by using special games based on these principles."

---

[29] Ibid. P. 23.

7.   Energy-saving motions of people and objects

A new engineering discipline concerning the "design of motions" is also needed. This science would develop *organizational principles* to reduce motion distances, save the floor area, arrange and organize things in a constrained space of a sophisticated factory. Gastev foresees that it would not be easy for organizational efforts to "overcome routine prejudices."

As a country of peasants, he wrote, Russia has a mentality that opposes precise organizational ideas. He added with hope, nevertheless, that "maybe it is here, in this virgin country, that truly radical ideas could materialize."[30]

These seven elements identified by Gastev should form the framework of a new culture to be struggled for right now. They are observation and recording; care for tools; biomechanics; bioenergetics; vocational psychology; training methodology and social engineering. If we do not win this battle with inertia and apathy, Gastev wrote, if our nation receives no careful education in new cultural setups, Europe and America will leave us far behind."

Who should be responsible for this "careful education"? Gastev believes this dissemination of culture should be entrusted to experts in scientific management, specifically the staff of TsIT, the institution he created. Indeed, the set of laboratories deployed at TsIT was an appropriate instrument to meet the above challenges. The **technological** laboratory designed the best tools for a given job; the **biomechanic** laboratory specified the character and duration of labor motions; the **physiological** laboratory was setting labor intensity limits and most effort-saving conditions of work; the **vocational psychology** laboratory selected the most appropriate workers; the **education and training** laboratory taught them labor skills; finally, the **social engineering** laboratory dealt with overarching issues of organization. Therefore, Gastev's concept of

---

[30] Ibid. P. 24.

new labor culture setups was at the core of the broad movement for scientific management emerging in Russia in the 1920s.

Gastev complemented his concept of cultural setups with that of new *work setups* to be cultivated in every worker, which would foster a drive for continuous improvement at workplace and at the enterprise as a whole. This idea was elaborated in his ground-breaking paper "Work setups,"[31] a sweeping treatise on scientific management. The scholar certainly realized that in the atmosphere of an economic collapse, in a country "completely cut off from the entire cultural world that has been creating technological progress," science was primarily expected to develop practical instructions on production planning, labor incentives and work efficiency to facilitate the recovery of industry.[32] *Gastev believed, however, that the country was facing a far greater challenge, since it had to undertake radical reengineering of the entire industrial system, including the worker as its most prominent production force.* The problem, he declared, was *to revamp production in such a manner that its very structure would incessantly call for innovation and improvement on a large scale as well as at workplace.*[33]

As we have already mentioned, Gastev thought that this daunting task could be addressed by means of a scientific management approach that would identify and formulate the basic principles and methods to transform work from "a heavy yoke" into "a positive creative process." It is highly significant that while discussing the "complete reorganization of labor" Gastev shunned any Marxist-Leninist rhetoric about the new "Communist paradise" where work would become "a delight". Do not lie to the masses, he said openly, by picturing a future "where we would live a happy and harmonious life. We are facing an era of hard work and

---

[31] См.: Gastev A.K. Work setups. *[Trudovye ustanovki]* / The Beginning of NOT. Forgotten Discussions and Ideas that Never Came to Life. [*U istokov NOT: Zabytye diskussii i nerealizovannye idei*]. Leningrad, 1990, P. 42-50.
[32] Ibid. P. 42.
[33] Gastev A.K. Ibid. P. 43.

extraordinary efforts... Our working life will be anything but Tolstoy's light exercise."[34] It will be appropriate to mention here that this phrase, like many others, would not be forgiven to this former member of the Communist Party.

Gastev and his colleagues certainly realized that labor could not automatically go through complete scientific reorganization. Such reorganization would require bold innovative research and decisive experiments based on a comprehensive concept of industrial management. Unlike later scholars, he realized that such a concept had to correlate with mainstream scientific management efforts abroad. According to Gastev, *to create an original theory one must critically review theoretical achievements and practical experience of industrialized countries.* The issue was largely a matter of common sense: Gastev was equally disgusted with the subservient approach to new Western theories that was (and still is) typical of certain Russian scholars, and the self-conceited arrogance by Yermansky and others who dismissed Taylorism, Fordism and other Western schools of thought as utterly irrelevant in Communist Russia.[35]

TsIT's research was inspired by its leader on the basis of these principles. Therefore, the Institute developed a distinctive and original concept of scientific management with due regard to the best discoveries of Western scholars such as Ford, Gilbreth, Gantt and, of course, F. Taylor.

While paying homage to Western European and American concepts of scientific management, Gastev stressed that so far they "have failed to... result in a conclusive methodology". For instance, Taylor made a major step forward by creating **the instruction card,** the ultimate standard for an operation that was handed to a worker by his supervisor and had to be strictly followed. However, Gastev

---

[34] Proceedings of the First All-Russian Initiating NOT Conference... Vol. 6. Moscow, 1921. P. 24.
[35] See: The Beginning of NOT. Leningrad, 1990, P. 43.

believed that Taylor "failed to create a certain *instructive methodology* which could be disseminated among broad masses to trigger incessant initiative."[36]

Gilbreth went much farther than Taylor. He investigated operation microelements, i.e. individual *work motions and techniques,* and used a rather limited body of evidence to develop some kind of a methodology based on standard work motions. "Again, however, Gilbreth never addressed the issue of providing the masses with a definitive methodology that would lead to permanent improvement of work techniques."[37]

Therefore, Gastev believed that whatever achievements could be credited to Taylor and Gilbreth were inadequate, if only because the concept of standards was a "frozen" norm that could become a routine and thus negate itself in the foreseeable future. Indeed, any standard is like "a snapshot of technological progress at a certain stage as applied to a specific work operation." It is but a *temporary* adaptation of a given industry to a given product or a given piece of equipment. Gastev, in contrast, pursued "a certain psychological and biological adaptation of a worker to *continuous improvement* of the operation itself and the relevant techniques… What we need to create is a general methodology of production that would cover literally every worker and encourage him – even when precisely following an instruction card – to come up with continuous improvement initiatives."[38] TsIT and its director was developing exactly this kind of a methodology, the one that would promote "a continuous drive for improvement" and continuous creativity in every modern worker. Moreover, Gastev believed that the elaboration of such a methodology (aimed at "inoculating every worker and others participating in production with a germ of labor improvement") should not be limited to TsIT. Rather, it should be a joint effort by all scientific management experts.

---

[36] Ibid.
[37] Ibid.
[38] Ibid. P. 44.

3. The "narrow base" concept

How should we start applying scientific management? Taylor and Ford, as is well-known, focused primarily on the workshop and enterprise levels. *TsIT concentrated on the individual workplace.* Gastev thought that the radical reconstruction of this primary manufacturing "cell" was an inevitable starting point for other organization models covering a workshop, an enterprise and an industry. He based his research strategy on the transition from microanalysis of motions, techniques and operations at workplace to macroanalysis of the enterprise as a whole. It was called **the narrow base methodology** and essentially meant that any scientific management efforts should begin with streamlining the labor of individuals, be they rank-and-file workmen or administrators. "Whatever organizational problems we are dealing with, - said Gastev at the All-Russian Congress of Engineers, - all our work in the long run boils down to a single objective, the development of new dexterity for workers and engineers alike."[39]

The "narrow base" strategy was heavily criticized by many contemporaries who accused Gastev of "utter primitivism", disregard for theory and lack of concern for enterprise management issues. In March 1924 P.M. Kerzhentsev, I.M. Burdyansky and other prominent advocates of the "broad base" approach to scientific management published "the platform of 17" that became a theoretical manifesto of the so-called "Communist NOT."[40]

Naturally, Kerzhentsev and his "group of 17" were much more skeptical about the potential of NOT under capitalism than Gastev. They believed, in full accordance with Marxist-Leninist clichés, that anarchy and competition pose insurmountable obstacles to the creation of a consistent scientific management

---

[39] "Vestnik inzhenerov", 1925, No.5. P. 139.
[40] NOT in the USSR. Theses for the 2nd NOT Conference. *NOT v SSSR. [Tezisy ko 2-y Vsesoyuznoy konferentsii po NOT]*. "Vremya", 1924, No.3.

system.[41] "Broad base" advocates claimed that NOT could be developed and widely applied only in the state-planned Soviet economy, that is, after the victory of the proletariat and nationalization of all means of production. "Once liberated from exploitation, NOT transforms from a tool of oppression into an instrument of conquering the forces of nature and facilitating human work."[42]

According to Kerzhentsev and his supporters, central planning must be used on a growing scale to unlock the true potential of NOT for the national economy. "Only robust planning skills at individual enterprises as well as across the economy, – claimed these teleologists of Russian scientific management, - only an ability to develop detailed and flexible plans... will put our economists on solid ground..."[43]

Needless to say that this philosophy was completely alien to Gastev who thought of it as empty rhetoric, "crude romanticism" geared to a fruitless quest for "Communist NOT as the philosophers' stone." Mind that hidden and open threats from communist scholars were anything but innocuous. For instance, Kerzhentsev interpreted Gastev's "theoretical blunders and deviations" as something leading to "dangerous practical consequences for NOT research, economic recovery and the truly proletarian position."[44] Burdyansky, the director of KINOT, was even more ominous: "To conclude this article, let me express confidence that an appropriate agency to coordinate all labor research in the country will be established in the near future to pay attention to the poison of reactionary ideology (in terms of both technology and politics) exuded by the Central Institute of Labor and change an abnormal situation when an institution financed by the proletariat conducts

---

[41] Ibid. P. 58.
[42] Ibid.
[43] Ibid. P. 60.
[44] Kerzhentsev P.M. Two NOT platforms: for discussion. *[Dve platformy po NOT: v diskussionnom poryadke]*. "Trud", 1924, February 22, No.43.

business that would be gladly paid for by the occupants of the Ruhr basin who support Russian counterrevolution."[45]

We see that TsIT became a target of major attacks. In Gastev's own words, the Institute was besieged, bullied and harassed by "a throng of enemies that kept disturbing its peaceful work with provocative discussions and complaints to the government. TsIT' main objective was to develop fundamental work setups, while Communist scholars were obsessed with plans and theoretical dogmas to be learned by heart... No wonder the development of NOT in this context becomes an almost religious quest for the philosopher's stone. i.e. the communist variety of scientific management."[46]

In most cases TsIT was criticized in a fairly non-constructive way. While Gastev and his colleagues invoked the "narrow base" approach to devise specific work techniques (say, for chiseling), their adversaries just declared their views on TsIT's ideas, that is, had a purely "literary" reaction to practical endeavors. For instance, a group of "Moscow communists" found it appropriate to attack Gastev and his colleagues because they ostensibly "a) reduce labor research to elementary muscular operations such as chiseling and filing, thereby distorting their relative importance in manufacturing and obfuscating the role of NOT in technological improvements and mechanization; b) underestimate the psychophysiological aspect of labor, ignore the issues of better work conditions and aim at increasing efficiency at the expense of occupational safety; b) idolize training that subjugates the worker to production processes and turns a live human being into a dumb robot without general skills or adequate education."[47]

---

[45] Burdyansky I.M. About a certain reactionary ideology. *[Ob odnoy reaktsionnoy ideologii].* "Kommunisticheskiy put", 1923, No.2. P. 67-68.

[46] Gastev A. Our NOT platform. Speaking notes for the conference of Moscow communists actively interested in NOT. *[Nasha platforma v oblasti nauchnoy organizatsii truda. Tezisy k konferentsii moskovskikh kommunistov, aktivno interesuyushchikhsya problemami NOT.]* "Pravda", 1923, January 11.

[47] The beginning of NOT. P.66.

Ya. Shatunovsky, a prominent party bureaucrat, also could not resist a temptation to join the crowd: "A. Gastev, his ideology and his Institute are just the scum on the wave crest of our Revolution. Though always on top, it's just scum anyway."[48]

As we see, Burdyansky, Kerzhentsev, Shatunovsky and others criticized TsIT mostly from the "class" position. Regrettably, this was an overwhelming trend. Occasional academic criticism was even more amusing, as evidenced by a sarcastic opinion by Professor Sokolov, who ridiculed the "narrow base" approach: "Take a shipyard building a dreadnought. Its tower alone needs a venerable 42,000 parts. With ten operations per part the total number of operations is 420,000. If research into just one operation, namely chiseling, could not be completed by TsIT in three years, because it brought about 64 separate problems, a full study of manufacturing one tower would require 1,260,000 years. This attitude is clearly wrong. The "narrow base" in such a situation becomes infinitely narrow. I do not mean that this approach has no value whatsoever. For instance, TsIT has used it to develop a training methodology, a nice achievement well worth the money. On the other hand, training has produced no tangible results at a single factory or government agency. The broad base method features none of these drawbacks because it aims at restructuring the entire enterprise."[49] As Gastev wittingly put it, Professor Sokolov could hardly see all the operations he was talking about, since this – at 10 minutes to study each operation – would require 24 years at eight hours a day without any days off.[50]

Such was the atmosphere in which TsIT had to develop its original school of thought. Fortunately, some government and party

---

[48] Shatunovsky Ya. Scientific management and its anarchist interpretation. *[Nauchnaya organizatsiya truda i ego anarkhistskoe vyyavlenie].* "Krasnaya nov", 1923, No.6. P. 252.
[49] Sokolov B.G. Two trends in NOT. *[Dva techeniya v NOT]* "Voprosy truda", 1924, No.1. P.68.
[50]The beginning of NOT. P. 69.

officials in the USSR were intelligent enough to appreciate the merits of TsIT's general methodology and the "narrow base" approach in particular. These included V.V. Kuybyshev who chaired the Second All-Union NOT conference that generally endorsed the efforts of TsIT and its director.

M.P. Tomsky, the Chairman of the All-Russian Council of Trade Unions (ARCTU) also was an ardent supporter "proud of TsIT, our brainchild nurtured by Gastev."[51] The leader of Russian trade unions unequivocally disclosed how Shatunovsky, Kerzhentsev and other "communist NOT experts" squealed on TsIT to the authorities, claiming that it "operates on a narrow scope", "deals with labor motions rather than general issues of labor management, thereby preserving obsolescent technologies in the country", and, most frightfully, has "no Party leadership." You can't systematically attack a non-communist, he said angrily, just because you happen to carry a Party card. "You comrades know how to *talk* beautifully, while Gastev is *an excellent NOT expert.* Commonplace talk is easy." "Certain comrades flash their Party cards and shout that the Institute has no Party leadership. However, we prefer a businesslike program and businesslike work to any Party affiliations."[52] This courageous support from a ranking government figure was very valuable. Regrettably, few people like Tomsky could be found among top government officials.

It should be stressed that the claims of Gastev's opponents were also *conceptually* wrong, particularly as they accused the scholar of "preserving obsolescent technologies" in the country. These critics ridiculed TsIT's efforts to streamline "primitive chiseling operations" and claimed that NOT would flourish only on the basis of "modern technology" which was "just about to arrive in Russia". Gastev and his colleagues, on the other hand, realized that in a country where 10 kilometers away from Moscow peasants were still wearing linden bark shoes and worship a nail like a

---

[51]Ibid. P. 94.
[52]Ibid. P. 95.

miraculous icon, NOT could and had to be implemented not only at advanced manufacturing facilities but in "any shed" and in any God-forsaken village. TsIT experts correctly assumed that labor management needs little investment yet can bring a fast and tangible return. "While a passive idealist would just be waiting for a machine to arrive as a savior that requires no skills whatsoever, - Gastev wrote, - we are realists. We rely on whatever equipment and work processes at hand rather than on some future progress."[53] Therefore, *TsIT formulated a productive approach to labor management based on the economic needs of the country as well as the actual opportunities available.* Indeed, advanced and backward forms of economy and culture were bound to co-exist in Russia for many years to come. Our system, Gastev said, "is not fastidious. It can apply to any axe or shaving plane just as well as... to the most precise of gauges."[54]

Gastev formulated "The Rules of Work" that forestalled many praxeological ideas of today and still sound useful. "Whether working at a desk, using a file in a locksmith's shop or tilling land, a worker has to cultivate self-control and gradually turn it into a habit."

Here are the basic rules for any kind of work.

1. Before starting a job, plan the final result and ponder over all your work techniques. Think of the main stages and carefully review the very first stage.

2. Do not start without all your tools and implements ready.

3. Keep no unnecessary things around your workplace (a machine, a workbench, a desk, the floor, a parcel of land) to spare yourself from hassle and wasting time on locating what you need.

4. All your tools and implements should be arranged in a certain (preferably permanent) order to be found easily.

---

[53]Ibid. P. 72.
[54]Ibid. P. 47.

5. Start your job gradually rather than abruptly. Your head and your body will soon adapt and start working. A sudden start would soon kill your stamina and ruin the job.

6. Some stages of a job require an exceptional effort or help from colleagues. Again, do not rush, take time to prepare your body and mind, to charge them, so to say. Give the job a try, feel your strength – and then do start.

7. Work should be as steady as possible, without any ebbs and flows. Otherwise you ruin the job and spoil yourself.

8. Take a convenient posture to avoid wasting your energy on maintaining it. Be seated, if possible. Otherwise stand with your legs apart and use a stopper to prevent skidding.

9. Rest during work. Hard work requires frequent rest periods. Easy work needs fewer rest periods but they must be regular.

10. Do not eat or have tea during work (at most, drink just to quench thirst). Smoke only during breaks.

11. If work does not progress well, do not be upset. Better take a break and do some thinking. Try again calmly, even slow down to restore self-control.

12. During one of the breaks, especially if the job proceeds slowly, clean up your workplace, put your tools in order, remove debris. Start again slowly but steadily.

13. Do not interrupt your work with anything but immediate work needs.

14. Showing a freshly done job to others is a bad habit. Have patience, get used to your success, hide your satisfaction. Otherwise in case of a failure next time you will get upset and start hating your work.

15. In case of a complete failure take it easy. Start all over again as if from scratch. Follow rule No.11.

16. Clean up after work and put your tools in order to start your work next time easier and feel happier.[55]

---

[55] Gastev A.K. How to work. Moscow, 1972. P. 33-34.

4. Features shared by management and manufacturing

Gastev's opponents grossly exaggerated his disregard for theoretical issues. We believe that the "narrow base" methodology and the social engineering approach described in the next paragraph enabled Gastev to arrive at a reasonably successful synthesis of the two key components of late Taylorism: (a) the microanalysis of work motions, techniques and operations (Gilbreth and others) and (b) the macroanalysis of the entire production process and its management (Gantt and others). Unfortunately, Gastev's contribution to the second area has never been adequately studied. Let us therefore discuss the *management* ideas of the Russian scholar in greater detail.

In contrast to eminent theoreticians such as Bogdanov or Yermansky, Gastev analyzed sector-specific rather than generic management processes. He clearly distinguished between the management of things and that of people as two separate research areas: "In the overall system... of movements the motions of man and their impact on others turned out to be a small but often the defining oasis." [56] At the same time he was sure that these two types of management shared certain features. In his own words, "A workman operating a machine is in fact an enterprise manager."[57] This enterprise features its own "departments" headed by the director:

Supplies (material)

Energy (motor)

Speed department (cogs and belts)

Adjustment (axis and spindles)

Tools (cutters and dies)

Accounting (revolution speed counters and feeding speed regulators)

Quality control (product measurement)

Management (apron with levers and cogwheels).

---

[56]Gastev A.K. How to work. P.26-27.
[57]Gastev A.K. Work setups. P. 208.

This machine also has its own record system based on job orders, defective product cards and time sheets, as well as its own "plan", "a system full of work motions rather than a static entity."[58]

Gastev believed that this approach led "to **the most democratic idea of management** when all personnel, even general help, are regarded as sort of "directors" running a certain mini-enterprise. "We completely abolish any division into the so-called subordinates and managers. We are stating that they often perform the same functions, even with routine jobs. We can identify "administrative" or management functions performed even by the least skilled worker. "[59]

Applying this idea to his own "narrow base" methodology, Gastev, therefore, treated general management issues at an enterprise, a sector or the entire national economy in terms of the workplace. He clearly demonstrated the value of this philosophy by identifying several functions that are inevitably performed by any worker at any workplace, be it a machine or the whole factory. These include a continuous series of actions involving "...planning-arrangement-processing-control-accounting-analysis-systematizing, planning-arrangement...".[60]

By extending this formula to the workman and the administrator alike Gastev essentially establishes a similarity between management of things (production) and management of people. Experience has been providing more and more evidence supporting Gastev's concept. In other words, the role of man in production can hardly be reduced to slaving the machine or a tool. The human being *manages* his tools in a highly individual way and imparts his personality to the entire industrial system. "Skilled

---

[58] Gastev A.K. TsiT's social banner [Sotsialnoe znamya TsIT]. The beginning of NOT. P. 103.
[59] Gastev A.K. Work setups. P. 212.
[60] Ibid. P. 269.

management of this system fosters true – that is, refined and business-like - administrative qualities in any worker."[61]

Accordingly, Gastev *indeed demonstrated a certain kinship between production and administration processes.*

The numerous – and often rabid – opponents of this concept were certainly wrong. While the similarity between production (management of things) and administration (management of people) is now fairly evident, it was an early version of *the core idea of sciences such as cybernetics, systems theory and praxeology. Research into administration in the context of production without opposing the two processes created an excellent foundation for streamlining and mechanization of the administration function at workplace as well as at an enterprise, a sector or the entire national economy.*

In other words, Gastev and his staff were following a very sound strategy. Similarity between management of things and management of people was a perfectly legitimate idea. On the other hand, *Gastev's concept included some other ideas and assumptions that could indeed have been challenged.*

We can hardly say the **similarity** between production and administration as a fundamental notion implied that Gastev and his colleagues completely ignored the **specific features of administration**. Nevertheless, these features were not central to their interests. Gastev and his colleagues did admit that the manager (who ideally should become a "social engineer" in TsIT's parlance) is largely responsible for the success of the industrial entity under his control as an integral "technological, biological and social" structure.

---

[61]Gastev A.K. TsIT's social banner [Sotsialnoe znamya TsIT]. / The beginning of NOT. P. 103.

Moreover, they formulated a number of important qualities of a good manager. For instance, Gastev thought he should be able "to launch a project in a tight situation, in a short time, with few tools and limited availability of materials; he should also be able to translate time to space and space to time."[62]

In Russia after the October revolution and the Civil war a good manager should also be **economically resourceful**. Gastev coined this term to describe a capacity for rapid and often unexpected economic maneuvering when time is limited, money is tight and top government bureaucracy issues endless orders and decrees.[63]

Socially, Gastev assumed that to create a general cultural background for management, a manager should be charismatic, tactful and polite as opposed to "outright rude".

Gastev also highly appreciated the art of teamwork. He contrasted "elementary everyday communism" ("which will take you nowhere") with the art of **fostering a work spirit in people** by means of "strong will and enthusiasm."

He also mentioned **the art of giving orders** that implied finding a common language with workers and creating the so-called social capital.[64]

Gastev's colleagues at TsIT also had some exciting ideas about managerial work. For example, A. Mikhailov, his disciple and close follower, singled out its key aspects such as 1) personal work ethics, 2) work strategy and 3) planning.[65]

---

[62]Gastev A.K. New cultural setup. *[Novaya kulturnaya ustanovka].* "Vremya", 1923, No.2. P. 12.

[63]Ibid. P. 13.

[64]Ibid. P. 13-14.

[65]Mikhaylov A. A few words about management. *[Koe-chto ob organizatorskoy rabote].* "Vremya", 1924, No.6. P. 22-26.

Without retelling this article or other TsIT publications we shall just note that they also contained many other ideas concerning managerial work. On the other hand, TsIT scholars were occasionally inconsistent in the interpretation of their own concept of a manager as primarily a "social engineer". For example, Gastev does contradict himself when he says that "We must eradicate whatever subjective psychological maneuvering of a supervisor to maintain the so-called good social relations in the workshop. Whether he deals with senior management or rank-and-file workers... he should use work schedules or another approved plan... Anyone who would continue with old rhetoric and ostentatious complaisance should be ruthlessly removed."[66]

It is surprising to see how Gastev suddenly refers to "social setups" such as tactfulness or courtesy as "rhetoric" and "ostentatious complaisance", scornfully talking of "so-called good social relations" to be maintained by a supervisor. This position is hard to agree with. Moreover, we believe that such inconsistency was indeed inherent to TsIT mentality. Rather than an unfortunate slip of the tongue, the above phrase testifies to *a gross exaggeration of similarity between labor and administration processes that subjugates management of people to management of things.* Gastev and his colleagues never cared for a specific issue of *differences* between these processes and limited themselves to the above-cited opinions on the appropriate managerial qualities. A scholar is certainly free to expand or reduce his area of interest and to focus on any problem of his choice. However, it appears that a focus on similarities between production and administration was not the real reason for Gastev and his school to pay so little attention to the **special nature** of management. We believe they simply thought that management has no real distinct features to talk about. Gastev's opponents could criticize him on these grounds rather than accuse him of ignoring the issues of management

---

[66]Gastev A.K. Improvements in manufacturing processes using TsIT's methodology (seamless implementation). [Ustanovka proizvodstva metodom TsITa (organicheskoe vnedrenie)]. Leningrad, 1927. P. 47.

completely. Once again, *Gastev never ignored management but treated it as a simple part of general manufacturing processes without any salient features.* "We see no difference, - he openly claimed, - between the so-called physical labor and the so-called intellectual labor, particularly management".[67]

Yet by completely (or almost completely) identifying the work of men managing a machine or a bench with that of administrators managing an enterprise or a sector, Gastev and his colleagues committed a **major theoretical fallacy.** *They grossly oversimplified the immeasurable complexity of management as such and reduced intellectual management efforts to a series of simple movements, operations and techniques.* "Managing a machine, - Gastev wrote, - determines the methods of managing any complex structure... You hold a file or a hammer – or bring the cutter closer to a blank - in a calculated, correct and precise way, exactly like you should organize production on a country-wide scale."[68] A man who can carefully organize his workplace, who knows about "the right posture, dexterity, precise movements and the tidy arrangement of materials, the man who passes the exam within his work zone, will be fit to brilliantly manage a workshop, a factory and, I would dare say, the whole country."[69]

This approach vividly echoes Lenin's dreams of a system "where **any kitchen maid** would be able to **govern** the country, *where every single worker in turn would participate in government – these have been the main slogans of our building efforts.*"[70]

How can kitchen maids, locksmiths and doormen be taught to govern? To this end, government should be continuously simplified and reduced to a set of elementary operations that can be mastered by anyone knowing the "four rules of arithmetic".

---

[67]Gastev A.K. Work setups. P. 47.
[68]Gastev A.K. TsiT's social banner [Sotsialnoe znamya TsIT]. P. 104-105.
[69]Ibid. P. 104.
[70] The beginning of NOT. P. 216.

While sharing some methodological aspects with Lenin's "scientific Communism", Gastev's idea of similarities between production and management processes turned out to be even more naïve than "Utopian socialism". Indeed, Utopian states were usually governed by intellectuals, enlightened industrialists, philosophers, aristocrats of the spirit, that is, a group of professional leaders better armed with information than the rest of the people. "Scientific Communism", much like Gastev, assumed that government should include primarily workers later aided by all "associated producers." This social ideal rests on a perverse concept that can hardly materialize in an industrial society, namely the combination of managerial functions with all other social duties of every citizen. Moreover, it is truly Utopian to suggest a government consisting of the most passive and the least informed group of society that is functionally tied to work implements.

Sadly, this theoretical fallacy had rather fatal practical consequences for the USSR. Gastev's concepts prompted massive promotion of workers and peasants to high managerial positions that required a deep and comprehensive knowledge of economics, psychology and sociology. Many thousands of factories, agencies and associations were managed by people without any idea of the "four rules of arithmetic" but with the major "advantage" of possessing a Party card. Moreover, for many decades they also governed a huge country – just think of Stalin, Kaganovich, Voroshilov, Khrushchev or Chernenko. Many top executives had no high-school diploma not to mention a college degree. Of course, it would be vulgar to put the blame on prominent scholars and personally honest people like Gastev and his many colleagues. They did exaggerate similarities between production and management, but people of entirely different morality and ideology cunningly took advantage of this mistake.

5. Social engineering as a science and a system

46

Gastev and his colleagues had intriguing ideas about scientific management which they called "social engineering", about its sources, its place in the system of sciences, its subject and laws. TsIT's director claimed with confidence that "it is right here, in our virgin country, one can act in the most revolutionary way possible"[71], meaning the domain of "precise ideas about organization". Gastev singled out four key sources of scientific management:

1. This science relies on priceless work and management experience "scattered through human history". First and foremost, it is the experience of artisan guilds in ancient and medieval history, that of trade unions (particularly in England) born during the "free industry" era, that of the army and, finally, the church.[72]

2. The second powerful source of scientific management, as noted above, are the global theoretical and practical innovations. All meaningful discoveries of Western NOT should be adopted by Russian management without any arrogance, albeit with a certain adjustment for the Russian environment and Russian ideas.

3. The third factor affecting the evolution of scientific management is the development of technologies and technology-related knowledge. Gastev noted that the technological revolution, particularly in industry, had a critical impact on the birth of scientific management, since "its logic was way more powerful than the most conservative resistance of administrators and workers alike"[73] The perfect "machinism", a movement towards complete automation and the ever expanding standardization of sizes and shapes of machined parts, tools and speeds has gradually led to a situation where "all too human gestures" of a live worker were "bound by a framework of calculated machine motions". The live work of man was doomed to succumb to the methodology of machine work, with its "analytics" that took care of minuscule values and rigid output standards. "Indeed, if Taylor were not born to measure work

[71]Gastev A.K. How to work. P. 52.
[72] Gastev A.K. Our objectives. / The beginning of NOT. P. 34-35.
[73] Ibid. P. 35.

times and decompose work into elements, he should have been ordered to be born."[74]

4. Last but not least, another crucial source for scientific management can be found in the achievements of sister sciences (e.g. technologies, psychophysiology, economics and education science) that must be correctly synthesized.

NOT progress in Russia, said Gastev, must take full advantage of all these sources without exception. "In our race to the future, - he wrote, - we want to be heirs to all the tragic and dark corridors of the past as well as the synthesizers of the present. We shall collect scattered historical experience of various classes, epochs and disciplines, enrich it with scientific achievements of our century, import knowledge from all continents and stitch it with the priority of methodical, rigorously calculated and automatic labor."[75]

Gastev, therefore, fully realized that the organization of labor and management was a sophisticated and multifaceted problem. While identifying, as already mentioned, **technology, psychophysiology, education and economics** as its key aspects, he did not merely mention these aspects but endeavored to sketch the main challenges facing each of them and identify specific problems to be addressed in the relevant areas of scientific management.

Economics appears to be far less important to Gastev than technology and education. On the other hand, *he succeeded in identifying certain major challenges for economics in the area of scientific management, claiming that so far its labor concepts had been highly abstract.* "This science has been making only limited use of precise accounting, and its working methodology has been too distant from a strict system of weights and measures. Yet now we are facing a challenge of arriving to clear-cut conclusions albeit in a very limited area." Insofar as relations between economics and NOT are concerned, Gastev focused on "economic incentives to labor",

---

[74] Ibid. P. 36.
[75] Ibid. P. 33-34.

meaning – and this has to be emphasized – physical work as well as management. This area, according to Gastev, had been particularly neglected. He noted that "the issue of economic initiative and incentives demands that the country be colonized by select talented managers. This is a social and economic challenge that we absolutely must address in very precise terms."[76]

Gastev made a real breakthrough by suggesting a new discipline *differing from all its predecessors.* "The problems we have just identified, - he wrote, - are a case for an entirely new science." Gastev thought that this new scientific management should be a **synthetic discipline.** At this point Gastev just outlined this idea. We believe, however, that the very fact of raising the problem of a **comprehensive** and "entirely new" discipline is a landmark in the history of scientific management. He called it "social engineering" and suggested that it must be a science of precise measurements, formulas and designs. "Notwithstanding sentimental philosophers that perplex us with the idea of elusive human emotions, we must fully mathematize psychophysiology and economics to use precise mood, agitation or fatigue factors, on the one hand, and the curves or straight lines of economic incentives, on the other hand."[77] Unfortunately, the author got somewhat carried away and failed to fully realize that social phenomena – including management – can only be formalized up to a certain limit.

Gastev tried to identify the key issues faced by the nascent scientific management. His top priority was *to precisely define its key components,* since "a mature science must incorporate a number of fundamental definitions."[78] Early scientific management, of course, lacked such rigorous definitions of categories and concepts. Secondly, he identified *the problem of laws,* since scientific management should deal with "laws of social mechanics and social management."[79] Identifying such laws is a key

---

[76] Ibid. P. 39.
[77] Ibid.
[78] Gastev A.K. How to work. P. 301.

challenge for a science at all stages of development, including the current stage. Regretfully, management laws have largely remained a mystery until the present day. In this context it is particularly interesting that Gastev divided scientific management laws into two large groups: (a) analytical laws, i.e. management trends that "split" the production process into separate acts, and (b) synthetic laws that tend to "aggregate" such acts to form sophisticated compositions.[80] This forgotten yet progressive idea should finally be used in current methodologies that deal with production management laws – albeit on a new and more advanced basis.

Gastev did not reduce social engineering to scientific management. He thought of it as a sophisticated *organizational system* brought to life by rapid industrial progress that features concentration of manufacturing and massive employment. Gastev believed that management becomes even more relevant with industriall development. It could be primitive in the world dominated by small-scale production; it plays a crucial role in the economy driven by machines and large factories. Today's mass production by large teams of workers can hardly be managed by traditional methods of yesteryear. Gastev suggests that this mass human organization should be treated as some kind of a machine. "We are coming to handle the task of organizing these large groups of people as engineers; we are investigating the material of this live machine to discard certain elements, sort these people and assign them to customized positions that help them develop manufacturing instincts.[81] In other words, "we apply engineering methods to a certain social task (i.e. organization – Author's note)."[82]

Along with "human groups", modern production involves *machine groups*. The organization of labor in society, therefore, is

---

[79]TsIT Organizational Calendar for 1924. *[Orga-kalendar TsIT na 1924 god].* Moscow, 1924. P. 53.
[80]Gastev A.K. How to work. P. 301.
[81] Gastev A.K. Production Setup Using TsIT Methodology. Moscow, 1925. P. 16.
[82] Ibid.

an involved and integrated combination of human group management with machine group management. These groups of "machine-humans", according to Gastev, result from the synthesis of biology and engineering. "And the calculated integration of certain human masses with the system of mechanisms will be nothing else but social engineering. "[83]

According to A. Festa, a TsIT fellow, "the machinist should tend to the machine, the foreman stay with his workers and the engineer oversee the foremen", that all work duties "from top to bottom should be precisely defined and specified," since "everybody must know exactly which values and factors are to be taken into account."[84]

Gastev's concept of social engineering, therefore, is of fundamental relevance. Using the human factor as a cornerstone and the "narrow base" of research into individual work movements and their elements in the course of developing "work setups", i.e. means to activate workers' potential, TsIT researchers developed the concept of work organization of society as a social engineering machine still controlled by the human factor.

6. Concepts shared by Gastev, Taylor and Ford

It is extremely interesting to compare Gastev's system with the impressive theories developed by F. Taylor and G. Ford and highly popular at the time (Gastev knew Ford personally and regularly exchanged letters with him). The three systems have much in common.

All these systems firmly reject the empirical approach to industrial management and challenge traditions and routine with

---

[83]Ibid. P. 17.
[84]Festa A. Fundamentals of industrial management. *[Osnovnye printsipy upravleniya predpriyatiyami].* "Organizatsiya truda", 1921, No.1. P. 21.

research. Subjectivism and quackery-like tools under systems gradually give way to a rational methodology that breaks the ice of obsolete, however customary, setups. *Taylor, Ford and Gastev believed that research was the essence of scientific management.* All the three scholars appropriately associated the birth of scientific management with the ever-increasing gap between the potential and the actual productivity of labor, and with the unacceptable waste of raw materials, finances and human resources. "The present system, – wrote, for instance, Henry Ford, - does not permit of the best service because it encourages every kind of waste—it keeps many men from getting the full return from service. And it is going nowhere. It is all a matter of better planning and adjustment."[85] He felt confident that the necessary planning could be achieved by scientific management. F. Taylor wrote that the scientific approach consists in organizing an enormous amount of traditional empirical knowledge into "laws, rule and even mathematical formulas," that replace the personal opinion of the individual worker.[86]

Gastev agreed. He thought of NOT as the streamlining of production methods based on carefully studied experience and requiring "continuous research into manufacturing or other work processes" as opposed to the predominantly empirical, semi-intuitive or, as he called it, "artisanal" approach.[87]

The NOT methodology, according to Gastev, includes the following stages:

1) preliminary analysis of the object and identification of its components;

2) selection of the best components that are later arranged in functionally interrelated series;

3) arranging the selected options according to ensure their most economical location in the manufacturing process;

---

[85] Ford H. My Life and Work. Garden City, NY, 1922. P. 15.
[86] Taylor F. Taylor on Taylorism (in Russian). Leningrad; Moscow, 1931. P. 55.
[87] Gastev A.K. Work setups. Moscow, 1973. P.270.

4) drawing a synthetic representation of the object under study.

Gastev assumed that any work methods could be modified only after a meticulous study. This logic echoes some ideas proposed by Taylor, Ford and other prominent management scholars but appears to go somewhat further.

Another feature that is common to Gastev, Taylor and Ford concepts is *the struggle for maximum efficiency of every individual element, however minuscule, of the manufacturing system to achieve productivity gains for every machine, mechanism and worker.* Gastev and his colleagues also suggested that the best (optimum) methods must be identified and applied at every stage of production.

Also, all the three systems were based on *scientific research of physical and personal production factors in the laboratory followed by practical tests.* Indeed, a researcher's key quality, according to Taylor, "is the capacity for expecting an outcome of his research for an indefinitely long time and continue work even if there are no results."[88] A similar attitude was typical of Gastev who reproached some participants of the First All-Russian NOT Conference of engaging in excessive "meditation". He thought of scientific organization as "a combat production task" and directly called for "stubbornness", "tenacity in work" and "overpowering oneself". "Scientific organization of labor, he said, - is a theory of tenacious work."[89] As shown above, Gastev himself and his colleagues at TsIT fully demonstrated their "stubbornness" in the defense against advocates of purely theoretical NOT such as Kerzhentsev and Shatunovsky.

---

[88] Taylor F. Taylor on Taylorism (in Russian). P. 11.
[89] Proceedings of the First All-Russian Initiating NOT Conference ... Vol. 6. P. 22.

The fourth common point is the *preliminary calculation and preparation of all production factors in time and space to accelerate and consolidate production processes as much as possible.*

All these systems also suggested *that workforce categories should be revised to restrict most workers to narrow special tasks (deep division of labor), the role of low and mid-level managers should be strengthened and more use should be made of training and various organizational tools.*

A few more general common points need to be mentioned. First of all, it is the treatment of the *labor intensity* issue. Taylor, as is well-known, presumed that a worker never operates at full capacity. With maximum productivity gains as his main target, Taylor recommended certain measures for labor intensification as a key factor of increasing efficiency. Hence his famous idea of a daily task, i.e. a clearly defined assignment that would certainly require some (usually major) efforts. In Russia the daily task system caused a controversial and sometimes outright confused reaction.

The overwhelming majority of Bolshevik-oriented NOT experts gave it a hostile reception as they deemed the system to be a new tool of squeezing value added. In fact, the tone for this discussion was set by Vladimir Lenin himself. In his famous paper "The 'Scientific' System of Squeezing Sweat" dating back to pre-revolutionary times (1913) the leader of the proletariat grieved over the plight of overstressed worker under Taylorism: "... hundreds of workers get the sack. Those who are left have to work four times more intensively, doing a back-breaking job. When he has been drained of all his strength, the worker will be kicked out.[90] To be fair, as early as in 1918 in his strategic brochure "The Immediate Tasks of the Soviet Government" he exercises a more benevolent approach by saying that it makes sense to apply "much of what is scientific and progressive in the Taylor system."[91] Even here, however, the vigilant Kremlin leader underscores that along with "a

---

[90] Lenin V.I. Complete Collected Works. Vol. 23. P. 19.
[91] Ibid. T. 36. P. 189.

number of the greatest scientific achievements" the system embodies "the refined brutality of bourgeois exploitation."[92]

P.M. Kerzhentsev, the perennial opponent of Gastev and TsIT as a whole, the chief ideological censor in the country, followed Lenin. He talked of "squeezing the maximum value added" and claimed that "productivity should be raised without intensification of labor."[93] O.A. Yermansky, another prominent Russian researcher known to be "unreasonably fond or workers" was an equally sworn enemy of Taylorism.

In contrast, Gastev and his colleagues advocated productivity gains as a matter of principle in a highly "pro-taylorist" way. In his speech at the First All-Russian NOT Conference Gastev frankly observed that personnel did not work at full capacity and, as Taylor put it, made only half-hearted efforts (today this phenomenon is called "restrictionism"). However, these workers are often unaware of their own potential. "When we come to the working masses and ask how much can a man produce in a minute... it turns out that no one knows."[94] Accordingly, labor intensity tends to be extremely low. This is why human physical and psychological potential must be identified, studied and utilized as much as possible.

Gastev distanced himself from the hypocritical and dogmatic "humanism" professed by Yermansky and his fellow Communists that in reality turned into unadulterated violence, forced labor and purges. He openly and honestly talked about comprehensive intensification of labor based on scientific data about the potential of the "human machine". Such a policy was appropriate in the economic and political climate that prevailed in the country in the early 1920s.

---

[92] Ibid. P. 189-190.
[93] The beginning of NOT. P. 115.
[94] Proceedings of the First All-Russian Initiating NOT Conference ... Vol. 6. P. 23.

A truly scientific intensification of labor, however, requires precisely what Taylor called "scrutinizing work". By carefully analyzing work motions and operations Gastev and his colleagues disintegrated each of them, as Taylor did before, into elementary components and used time studies and other tools to remove all "erroneous", "extraneous" and useless motions and optimize the remaining best elements.

The next aspect that related Gastev's system to Taylorism and Fordism was *the commitment to the division of labor in management.* Taylor, as is well-known, rejected the linear system of management under which every worker reported to his immediate supervisor. He suggested an alternative functional management organization that replaced the only supervisor or workshop director controlling everybody and everything with functional bosses. Each of them was responsible for a certain area (mounting blanks on machines, work speed control or maintenance). Each worker, therefore, received instructions and help from several highly specialized direct supervisors. Gastev and his colleagues were also skeptical of linear management and argued for the division of labor in management. In the early 1930s, when a massive campaign started in the country against "functionalism", Gastev had to yield to brutal force and change his mind (which, unfortunately, did not save him).[95]

Yet another idea shared by Gastev and Taylor was that of *setting up a kind of headquarters at enterprises, i.e. planning and distribution offices* that were believed to be critical to efficient production, and *the introduction of payment schemes based on individual output rather than the output of the worker's team.* A number of other common concepts could also be identified.

---

[95] Gastev A. Organizational ideas of the XVII Party Congress and TsIT's work. *[Organizatsionnye idei XVII s'ezda i rabota TsIT].* "Organizatsiya truda", 1934, No.2. P. 7.

If Gastev and his colleagues borrowed so much from Taylor, Ford and other Western scholars, one may wonder whether the TsIT school was in fact independent or original. Should we agree with Kerzhentsev who exclaimed pompously: "Oh Taylor, I recognize you! TsIT has learned well your attitude to the worker – with condescension, with some money in the fist, with mysterious formulas and little confidence in his consciousness!"[96] Should we, in the spirit of such opinions, discuss "Russian Taylorism" rather than Gastev's original school of thought?

Certainly not. Gastev and TsIT, his brainchild, left a unique footprint trace in the history of global scientific management. As we have seen, they developed a distinct methodology and theory, a kind of a "humanistic" challenge to Taylorism and Fordism. We think that all the above-mentioned shared features cannot and should not disguise the very distinct nature of this system.

7. Singularity of Gastev's system.

What is so unique about Gastev's system? As is well-known, Taylorism was based on workshop labor organization, primarily by means of time studies, training, a differential payment system and functional management. Fordism, on the other hand, proposed a new approach to the organization of production, including continuous manufacturing processes, a maximum division of labor, mechanization of manufacturing and transportation up to the conveyor belt system, recycling of all waste and so on.

Both Taylorism and Fordism, however, completely ignored Gastev's fundamental ideas of *"socialization of labor processes"* and *the key role of the human factor.* In contrast to Taylor, who was primarily concerned with organization as such, and Ford, who focused on technologies, Gastev and TsIT, with all due respect to

---

[96] Kerzhentsev P. Two platforms on NOT: For discussion. [Dve platformy po NOT: v diskussionnom poryadke.] "Trud". No. 41. February 20, 1924

both American systems, believed that the human factor was the core of manufacturing. TsIT fellows were in fact the first NOT researchers in the world who established the leading role of man in production and claimed that it was man who largely determined the success of the entire business.

The ultimate objective of research for nascent Western scientific management was to determine a certain standard for every operation, method or motion that should be used – though not necessarily understood by the worker who applies this (as Gastev put it) "frozen norm". The "standardization principle" brought to its logical conclusion tends to negate itself by turning into a dogma rather than a guide to action and by preserving obsolete work methods. Accordingly, it ceases to foster better organization and becomes a burden for a given operation, a given motion and production as a whole.

Gastev and his colleagues found a way to address this contradiction. They believed that *discussions of a priori norms and social conservatism of workers who ostensibly reject everything new make little sense; what had to be developed was the psychological and biological adaptation to continuous improvement of work operations and the method to learn the art of accelerating work.* First of all, a methodology was needed to teach all factory personnel the general rules of manufacturing. While any workman was expected to closely follow the rigid instruction card, Gastev's methodology also assumed a rather wide range of personal initiatives to change norms and standards. Again, he thought of this methodology as "inoculating every worker and others participating in production with a germ of labor improvement." This was the heart of Gastev's famous idea called "the work setup". No Taylor, Gilbreth or anybody else ever thought of a methodology that would "infect" the masses and encourage continuous initiative. Gastev proudly noted that he "aims at activating the working masses, planting the devil of invention in their souls, the devil that incessantly forces them to try, to adapt, to be active and agile in all situations."[97]

Gastev suggested that research into scientific management be brought as close to manufacturing needs as possible. While accepting standards as a certain element for a given plant, he thought they were less important than the capacity for fast restructuring of production processes and the appropriate retraining. Indeed, the scholar and his disciples strived for more than simple standardization. Their main objective was to define the entire evolution of an operation from the most primitive to the most efficient. The "setup principle" as interpreted by TsIT meant developing a series of ever improving setups from elementary human motions to a perfect work technique.

It is important to note that TsIT scholars wanted to apply the work setup concept to human culture in general rather than just manufacturing. As Gastev put it, "we carry our work setup beyond the factory gate. We see our environment as a series of setups where we can occasionally create temporary standards. In any event, our setup method can do only one thing – continuously revolutionize everything within and beyond the factory. Even issues of everyday life or general culture call for the use of the setup system, the so-called cultural setup, which forces us to construct certain series."[98]

We trust that Gastev and his colleagues made a major step forward from Taylorism, Fordism and the Western school as a whole, since they applied a *fundamentally new approach to the assessment of the worker by regarding him not as an object of research but as a creative person whose perception of the world is a key element of potential productivity gains.* Taylor's school and other systems paid scant attention to psychophysiological aspects of work. In contrast, TsIT researchers, who also studied the

---

[97]The beginning of NOT. P. 48.
[98] Gastev A.K. Work setups. "Organizatsiya truda", 1924, No.1. P.24-25.

geometry and energy of work motions to achieve maximum efficiency and exclude all unnecessary elements, never ignored the man, his health and work conditions. While Taylor and Ford regarded the worker as "just a machine", TsIT believed that workers were "live machines", i.e. sophisticated human organisms. A. Bruzhes, a senior expert at TsIT, stressed that scientific management studies must take into account human physiological processes to eliminate unproductive activities and dramatically increase efficiency. NOT, according to Bruzhes, should carefully study both the "live machine" and all the factors that affect its functioning.[99]

On the other hand, Gastev and TsIT never reduced NOT to physiological studies. Moreover, their concept of NOT's physiological aspects was very different from the "physiological optimum" theory developed by O.A. Yermansky and quite popular at the time. Gastev, who was highly critical of this theory, noted that "the TsIT approach" can in no way be replaced with "semi-Utopian dreams of the optimum" and "daydreaming about the unacceptability of work intensification." The scholar firmly believed that human psychophysiological capacities are dynamic rather than "frozen", i.e. given once and for all.

Hence his conclusion that *physical and psychological capacities require continuous training* in areas such as power of observation (training the sensory organs, especially the eye and the ear), willpower, motion culture (dexterity, speed of response), figurative powers (capacity for graphic or verbal description), feeling of time (accounting for time spent), and so on. All this, as Gastev and his colleagues believed, would activate the human factor as much as possible while saving the energy and protecting the health of workers who would judiciously spend their efforts. At the same time Gastev and his school were lukewarm and even skeptical about psychotechnics (vocational psychology) that dealt

---

[99] Bruzhes A. et al. The live machine. *[Zhivaya mashina]*. Moscow, 1924.

with problems of vocational selection. More details on this issue can be found in the next section.

Chapter 2. TsIT and education.

1. Training as an alternative to psychotechnics.

Teaching or training, as we remember, was the second component of the "triune mechanism" for the emergence and development of scientific management. Based on Gastev's central idea of the human factor's key role in the structure of the "social engineering machine", TsIT's professionals paid major attention to the issues of professional training and retraining. Moreover, by mid-1920s *TsIT considered training and retraining* to be the **most important** of all its objectives. As N. Levitov, a TsIT fellow, wrote: "This is the main job of TsIT, an unusual factory that produces trained workers bursting with organizational and production energy."[100]

While addressing this major issue, Gastev and his colleagues arrived at a most interesting and original *setup (engineering) method of training with a strict "gradual release" of knowledge, a proud achievement of Russian scientific management that came to enjoy global recognition (see below).* Gastev noted that this method "was of importance as a certain reform of training, education and improvement of workforce", while TsIT, accordingly, became "a new type of a special enterprise dealing with mass production of workers."[101]

What is so unique about the setup method? We have already noted more than once that Western founders of scientific management usually regarded the human worker as something **static,** not as "raw material" to be processed but as a fixed element of the manufacturing process that was good for performing certain limited work functions but incapable of doing anything else. These

---

[100]Levitov N. TsIT's method of workforce training. *[Metod TsITa dlya podgotovki rabochey sily.]* "Voprosy truda", 1926, No.1. P. 18.
[101]Gastev A. TsIT as a research facility. *[TsIT kak izyskatelnoe sooruzhenie].* "Organizatsiya truda", 1928, No.1. P. 19.

ideas triggered (first in the West and later in Russia) the explosion of psychotechnical methods of personnel selection that heavily relied on the innate qualities of a prospective worker.

In contrast, Gastev brought forth his own **dynamic** concept. He came up with *a hypothesis of almost limitless potential of human psychophysiological development* as the core of the unprecedented *TsIT training methodology,* **the system of fostering human talents.**

We have already noted that Gastev had reservations about psychotechnical research. His skepticism, of course, should certainly not be exaggerated. He did acknowledge that some innate talents are indispensable in certain professions. Indeed, one can hardly imagine a composer without an ear for music. Gastev never flatly rejected any methods of selecting people for recruitment and promotion. Moreover, he asked some TsIT scholars (such as the already mentioned N. Levitov) to take part in research into occupation fitness understood as "a certain combination of abilities, inclinations, knowledge and skills that results in a fast and accurate performance."[102] This definition means that people unfit for a job may lack talent, knowledge or skills or otherwise fail to meet physical or psychiatric health criteria, including age.

How, then, ca occupational fitness (or unfitness) be judged? How can the combination of abilities, inclinations, knowledge and skills needed for a certain job be evaluated? These (usually subjective) judgments are based on documents (applications, references, forms or degree certificates), interviews and observations. TsIT researchers were wary of such evaluations, however, and maintained that "subjective opinions as a measure of success are not reliable since their practical value depends on personal views of the evaluator, the qualities being evaluated and the evaluation methods."[103]

---

[102]Levitov N. Management assessment of workers for hiring and promotion. *[Otsenka administratsiey sluzhashchikh kak osnova dlya naima i vydvizheniya.]* "Voprosy truda", 1926, No.5-6. P. 67.

Therefore, Gastev and his colleagues paid certain tribute to psychotechnics as a discipline designed to work out methods of *objective* evaluation of occupational fitness and even thought that such methods "should be used in all instances where they were experimentally validated."[104] Yet they urged to remember that psychotechnical tests have obvious limitations and, while minimizing the subjectivity of evaluations, cannot eliminate it altogether.

Gastev and his colleagues saw much more promise in an idea that abilities, inclinations, knowledge and skills are something **trainable** rather then set once and for all, i.e. they can be **developed** by training. The main challenge, therefore, is **to devise a method of vocational training to expand human capabilities as much as possible.** "We keep urging people to develop their talents, go for training and improve their skills. - Gastev wrote. – We revolutionize modern biology and assert that man has a wealth of capabilities, thousands of opportunities for adaptation, training and success. That's why we are so opposed to psychotechnicists: *training rather selection is our top priority* (the italics are mine – Author)."[105] As we see, Gastev does not dismiss psychotechnical methods as fundamentally erroneous or unnecessary; he just regards them as subordinate.

TsIT believed that traditional training methods used by vocational schools and colleges were woefully obsolete and failed to meet the needs of the rapidly recovering economy that was embracing new technologies and urgently required a skilled workforce. Vocational schools were often requested to participate in manufacturing, which essentially turned them from educational

---

[103]Levitov N. Impartial grounds for hiring and promotion. *[Ob'ektivnye osnovaniya dlya naima i vydvizheniya sluzhashchikh.]* "Voprosy truda", 1926, No.11. P. 33.
[104]Ibid. P. 39.
[105]Gastev A. TsIT's social banner./ The beginning of NOT. P. 105.

establishments into second-rate auxiliary factory shops. Thus any education of workforce was reduced to the so called "hands-on training", with students "spending most of their time on meaningless tasks devoid of any educational value."[106] Such "training" produced workers who "might know hundreds and thousands of minute details of a particular process but have no idea of general skills of their trade even after several years of schooling."[107]

Instructors at vocational schools were often professionally unfit people without adequate methodological or educational background.

The most disturbing aspect, however, was the lack of an efficient method for fast and high-quality mass vocational training, a method that would teach professional skills as well as foster incessant creativity at workplace. The development of such a method at TsIT was a comprehensive process including extensive experiments in biomechanics, bioenergetics and, to an extent, psychotechnics. Eventually TsIT did create its own methodology.

The essential idea behind this method is **the "machinization" of work motions made by the "live assets" of a factory.** By selecting and refining the necessary motions TsIT's approach sought to achieve a perfect command of these motions, i.e. complete automatism. As a result, "nervous energy would be released to stimulate initiative" and "infinitely enhance the power of a given individual."[108] The more automatism is acquired by the worker, the greater are his capacities for addressing new problems. "The principle of machinization or biological automatism, - Gastev wrote, - should extend very far, even to the so called intellectual faculties."[109]

---

[106]Labutin A., Mikhaylov A. Industrial training with the use of TsIT methodology. *[Proizvodstvennoe obuchenie po metodike TsITa].* "Vremya", 1924, No.8. P. 20.
[107]Ibid.
[108]Gastev A.K. Work setups. P. 46.
[109]Ibid.

Gastev certainly did not mean the simple automatism that involves repeated simple motions and eventually leads to "hibernation" or "hypnosis". If a process incorporates an ever increasing number of automatic motions, if a man "gets used to the growing number of new variables, he becomes an unbounded creator."[110] For instance, a presumably simple operation such as chiseling "reveals the depth of imagination and memory elements in the course of work, provides a key to the structure of the so called intellectual work... we think of it as an enormous chain of consecutive elements simple and complex, as the creation of powerful automates, their incorporation into groups, a continuous renewal of these automates by means of new reactions."[111] Research into chiseling at TsIT made it possible to refine the training system and set an objective of "educating a singular **new high-speed man** who would react fast, always be alert yet spend as little nervous energy as possible."[112]

This training system was supposed to apply to thousands and thousands of workers across the country. Briefly, its main objective was to impart **a new motion culture** "that would precisely define both the motions and the psychological aptitude needed by the worker."[113] Also, it was designed to develop the system of **work setups** with the help of templates, leaders and drivers. After thoroughly refining the simplest work elements TsIT researchers moved to the highest stage of training (**organizational and operational training)** in the field, where "each element is tested for quality and speed."[114] Organizational training was aimed at fostering obedience rather than supervisory capacities. Gastev held that only an obedient worker makes a good manager.

---

[110]Ibid.

[111]Ibid. P. 47.

[112]Gastev A.K. TsIT's social banner [Sotsialnoe znamya TsIT]. P. 105.

[113]Gastev A.K. Production Setup Using TsIT Methodology: consistent implementation. *[Ustanovka proizvodstva metodom TsIT (organicheskoe vnedrenie)].* Moscow, 1925, P. 8-9.

[114]Ibid. P. 23.

Organizational training, he wrote, is the only way to test one's abilities, "to check responsiveness, automatism and the skill to go down to business right away without unwarranted family sentiments."[115] Only a worker trained to be obedient can be allowed to perform more sophisticated organizational, managerial and planning functions. This principle was the cornerstone of Gastev's new discipline, "the training pedagogy", that implied precise calculations taking into account every small detail.

At the same time Gastev perfectly realized that the new work culture cannot rely solely on "obedience" that turns a worker into a "cog" in an enormous manufacturing mechanism. Any work, he insisted, required creativity, a craving for invention, design and improvement. The worker himself should ponder over each of his motions and strive for their streamlining and improvement.

TsIT's system of developing the motion culture, learning work procedures and ways to improve the production process was complemented with special **psycho-training** to foster the power of observation, recording capacities, swift response and automatism. Unfortunately, Gastev said, our inherent psychological laxity is often clouded in general philosophical phrases that lack simple logic and give no chance to find out whether it is something, or other or both. "Psychologically, we always pretend to stand out from the crowd – just as some passionate revolutionaries who never comb their hair."[116] He advocated persistent, rigorous and patient psychological training that would not be completely free of compulsion.

The final step in TsIT's method was a **time self-study** where the worker would record the time spent of a given operation in his instruction card.

---

[115] Gastev A.K. The revolt of culture. P. 32.
[116] Ibid. P. 31.

2. Setup vocational training.

The *setup vocational training method* centered on the figure of the instructor. He was responsible for defining the type of training and work as well as for continuous control, monitoring and guidance. He was also to make his students focus on literally everything: the right stand, the way of holding the tool, the efficient position of hands, and, most importantly, the precision of motions. In other words, he was supposed to establish work setups and inoculate the student with that same "work germ" mentioned above. "Training is our principal tool, - Gastev wrote. – Instructors that are scattered all over the factory as proactive trainers also do a job of everyday inspectors and troubleshooters. The instructor monitors all setups, he directs and continuously initiates new perfect setups. We believe that namely the introduction of mass training in Soviet Russia... evokes *restless creativity* in the working masses."[117]

The setup method of training and retraining was based on several methodological rules (principles) reflecting the theoretical achievements of TsIT.

Principle 1. Organization of work environment or social engineering. Workers should be provided with a system of organizational and biological setups (based on engineering and biological research) that would allow them to merge seamlessly with machines and equipment, turning the factory into a true social engineering entity that would function as rhythmically, precisely and flawlessly as a machine tool.

Principle 2. Detailed analysis of work processes. Any work should be broken down into details, operations, simple and complex elements that make it possible to reconstruct the entire process. For instance, TsIT analyzed the metal-working industry to identify three types of works: (1) manual operations with tools, (2)

---

[117]Gastev A.K. Work setups. P. 49.

machine tooling and (3) assembly. Manual operations with tools were divided into strike and pressure operations. Machine tooling included operation and mounting. Assembly included bracketing, adjustment and putting parts together (or dismantling them).

Principle 3. Any work is a stream of operations, any complex operation is a set of individual operations that, in turn, consist of techniques incorporating simple and complex elements.[118] Gastev himself developed an "analytical setup diagram" for chiseling, an example of meticulous analytical work that was used for training factory instructors.

Principle 4. Work as a dynamic phenomenon. Workers should be trained to aim at ever faster work and higher precision of operations. Here TsIT identified two main objectives. The *bioenergetic objective* was to "inoculate the modern man with a special urge for continuous biological improvement, repairs and adjustments". The *orga-energetic objective* means providing man with "the highest degree of organizational condensation and methods of organizing his entire life."[119]

Principle 5. Detailed work regimens. During the training process all work periods and breaks were strictly determined in accordance with the worker's biological factors and the work environment. For instance, training sessions for instructors in the strike operations workshop started with 30 seconds of work followed by a 1 minute break; these periods gradually became longer at the next stages. In the pressure operations workshop 1 minute of work was followed by a 1 minute break initially; at the final stages of work these periods increased to 15 and 3 minutes respectively. A worker who felt exhausted before the work period ended could sit down to have some rest; in case of a sickness he would be sent to a doctor.

---

[118]Levitov N. TsIT's method of workforce training. *[Metod TsITa dlya podgotovki rabochey sily.]* "Voprosy truda", 1926, No.1. P. 20.
[119]Ibid.

Principle 6. Gradual increase in complexity of instructions. The main challenge faced by TsIT instructors was to develop a series of setups based on a gradual transition from coarse and primitive hand motions to the use of tools and further to sophisticated combinations of higher nervous activity with modern machinery.

Principle 7. The "narrow base". The training methodology was to rely upon careful "microscopic" studies of several typical techniques and operations; a deep study into one of them provided a key to learning a number of others. These typical "delegating" operations (such as chiseling and filing in the strike operations shop and the pressure operations shop respectively) shared several characteristic elements with other operations. Despite fierce criticism, the "narrow base" principle was consistently applied to all TsIT training courses. "We support the narrow base, - Gastev wrote, - and today we have 300 times as much confidence in it as at the time this principle was proclaimed. The narrow base is an integral and deep method that has been only strengthened by our experience and all the arguments we had with our opponents."[120]

Gastev's methodology proved to be highly efficient in mass vocational training, a top priority area at that time. It allowed to train a skilled worker in 3 to 6 months as opposed to the 3-4 years at a typical vocational school. TsIT was requested to use its method to train 10,000 workers in a year, at a cost of 1.2 million rubles. Similar training at vocational schools cost 24 million rubles.[121] TsIT and Gastev personally cannot be praised enough for the solution of this critical problem of the economy.

---

[120]Gastev A.K. Production setup using TsIT methodology. P. 54.
[121] Berkovich D.M. The evolution of scientific management in industry. Moscow, 1973. P. 86.

Chapter 3. Consultations, implementation and practical innovation

1. Institutional framework.

As already mentioned, consultation, implementation and practical innovation are the third pillar of Gastev's "triune" mechanism for the foundation and development of scientific management. Let us dwell on the institutional framework for these functions at TsIT.

In this area TsIT used *practical innovation bodies such as pilot stations, orga-stations, organization bureaus, practical innovation bureaus and special self-financing trusts.* Relatively little has been written about these entities in the literature though they were responsible for most practical innovation efforts in work and management. A.Z. Goltsman, one of Gastev's associates, wrote that "when senior management enthuses over modern innovation ideas, while lower organizations are wallowing in the swamp of purely Russian technological and cultural backwardness,"[122] these bodies actually initiated and encouraged innovation and restructuring.

Let us briefly describe the history of these units and demonstrate their role in the early development of scientific management.

The history of such special innovation units may be conveniently divided in three stages. From 1921 to 1923 they were mostly established by TsIT (and other research centers supporting Gastev's idea) as *pilot stations* that could be called practical innovation centers in the strict sense of the word. . A pilot station was a unit established by a NOT research institute at a factory or

---

[122] Goltsman A.Z. At the threshold of innovation. [*U poroga ratsionalizatsii.*] "Khozyaistvo i upravlenie", 1926, No.3. P. 13.

institution to conduct monitoring, experiments and research into management practices. Pilot stations were also expected to help implement their own recommendations. Their staff included research fellows and they were often headed by prominent scholars.

TsIT established the first pilot station at *Elektrosila No.5* factory in 1921. The second one at *Tsentroyuz* followed the same year.[123] Since 1922 such units were created by TsIT at textile plants of the Trekhgornaya manufaktura, at the Orekhovo-Zuevo trust, the Bogoroditsk-Shchelkovo trust, the Khleboproduct JSC, the Gudok newspaper, at branches of Sotsstrakh and elsewhere.

These pilot station performed the following functions:

- research into administration and production mechanisms at the organization and its departments;
- identifying ways to increase management efficiency;
- developing a lean management system;
- participation in the implementation of their recommendations.[124]

To reorganize a plant or an institution, TsIT recommended that pilot stations start with a process review, a kind of organizational intelligence gathering that would provide comprehensive instructions on what can be changed and in which order. This work started with selecting an area for innovation. E. Salomonovich, a TsIT fellow in charge of pilot stations, wrote: "To address strategic problems we need outstanding synthetic minds. Down-to-earth NOT, however, requires that a specific area be chosen within an organization that promises real results, while remaining a typical component of the whole. In this case any conclusions for this small area can be applied to many other areas that eventually need to be streamlined."[125]

---

[123] The beginning of NOT. P. 59-60.
[124] " Voprosy organizatsii i upravleniya ", 1922, No.1. P. 24.

Once the area is selected and clear objectives of innovation are established, TsIT recommended a detailed study of its small components, elements and simple operations.

The next stage involved research into three aspects of individual elementary operations:
- efficiency (what is to be done, what has been done, how precise is the operation, how much time it takes and how tiring it is for the worker);
- statics (human and physical factors of production such as tools, implements, blanks and raw materials; their location in space; work environment including lighting, heating, clothing and labor protection);
- dynamics (individual techniques involved, distribution of techniques over time, speed of operations, alternation of work and break periods, absolute and relative use of time, taking photos of the working day and so on).
   Such a detailed critical review of operations reveals the flaws of current practices. A new reorganized workflow scheme is then developed and a new instruction card is written.[126]

At this point research gives way to the final – and the most challenging – stage, i.e. implementation. Its success largely depends on personal qualities of the innovator and the management of the enterprise. The key factor here is discipline. Some TsIT fellows claimed that the work of pilot stations "may easily be called a struggle for discipline" and "for the introduction of measures that are essential to any system."[127] E. Salomonovich thought that the pilot stations' main objective is to ensure that all employees and departments never fail to discharge their duties in a fast and precise

---

[125] Salomonovich E.D. Industrial restructuring practices. *[O praktike rabot po reorganizatsii promyshlennykh predpriyatii]*. "Predpriyatie", 1923, No.1. P. 48.
[126] Ibid. P. 49.
[127] Salomonovich E.D. Office work setup. *[Ustanovka raboty v uchrezhdeniyakh.]* "Organizatsiya truda", 1924, No.8-9. P. 37.

manner. Mismanagement can hardly be explained by a lack of planning. In fact, a multitude of wonderful plans, projects and programs have been developed lately. "What we are lacking is... a clear understanding of the mysterious art of giving orders with authority, ensuring their execution and moving on with further organizational plans."[128]

Unfortunately, a close cooperation between enterprises and pilot stations failed to materialize. In legal terms, such a station was not a part of the host enterprise. Also, practical innovation that benefited the enterprise was far less of a priority for the station than research and theoretical studies.[129]

Nevertheless, pilot stations were highly instrumental to the advance of scientific management. E. Rozmirovich compared them to "focal points where the fundamentals of the new science were conceived and forged. They were the main source of information for research centers that systematized their observations to benefit scientific management."[130]

Since enterprises did not care much for pilot stations that paid little attention to practical innovation, TsIT, as it appears, was prompted to seek alternative institutional arrangements. Pilot stations were gradually converted to "orga-stations" and "organizational bureaus". This started the second period in the history of factory-based practical renovation entities (1923-1925).

---

[128] Salomonovich E.D. Execution of work. [Ispolnitelstvo]. "Organizatsiya truda", 1924, No.4. P. 37.

[129] As a result of such reforms an institution would occasionally find itself "equipped with a fairly elegant theoretical system that was completely irrelevant and inconvenient in practice". (Pshigoda G. The team method of restructuring for government agencies. *[Kollektivnyy metod provedeniya ratsionalizatsii apparata gosuchrezhdenii]*. "Hozyaystvo i upravlenie", 1926, No.1. P. 65).

[130] Rozmirovich E. The present and future of management departments at government agencies. *[Sovremennoe sostoyanie i perspektivy rabot orgbyuro v gosudarstvennykh uchrezhdeniyakh.]* "Tekhnika upravleniya", 1925, No.4. P. 4.

To an extent, orga-stations were free of drawbacks inherent to their predecessors since they were established by TsIT (and similar institutions) at enterprises and agencies with a direct task to improve management. Host enterprises were much more interested in such entities. While orga-stations still reported to TsIT rather than the enterprise, their workplans met the needs of the host who paid TsIT for its services. In contrast to pilot stations, therefore, orga-stations were concerned primarily with practical innovation rather than academic research.

For example, this is how a TsIT orga-station at the Sobolevo-Schelkovo textile plant operated as described by its director F. Kuteyshchikov. His experience is of considerable value in our "time of troubles."

One of the objectives set by the orga-station in consultation with the plant management was "to develop a streamlined management system including standards for the relations between individual elements of management... to make every employee aware of his rights and responsibilities and ensure that the administration has an opportunity for efficient management."[131] To this end, TsIT also defined principal criteria for an efficient management system:

1.No management is possible without discipline that, according to Kuteyshchikov, means the manager's confidence in accurate and fast execution of all his orders.

2.Every worker should know his exact rights and responsibilities.

3.The ultimate authority to address any issue must be clearly defined.

4.Final authority should be delegated to rank-and-file as often as possible. This principle is especially noteworthy since it confers the power of decision-making and initiative on employees.

---

[131] Kuteyshchikov F. Management at textile enterprises. *[Voprosy upravleniya v tekstilnykh predpriyatiyakh].* "Organizatsiya truda", 1924, No.1. P. 57.

Today, as is well-known, it is a fundamental concept of scientific management.

5.Automatism, i.e. procedures under which the rights and responsibilities of every worker are defined so clearly that most issues can be addressed by rank-and-file without any authorization from senior management.

6.Issues under the exclusive jurisdiction of senior management should be clearly defined.

7.Every worker should deal with only one precisely defined business as much as possible.

8.Every employee should bear responsibility for the precise and timely execution of his duties and orders from administration.

The orga-station reviewed the actual management system at the plant to find out where the above criteria of efficiency were not met.

Discipline, for example, was studied by looking into (a) the time needed for orders from the director to reach the executors, (b) the ratio between executed and unexecuted orders and (c) the delays in executing orders by executors and intermediaries.

A detailed study demonstrated that only 60—70% of orders were executed. The remaining 30—40% were either ignored or simply lost in the intermediate links of the system and never reached the workers. It was also found that it took orders an incredible time of 3—7 days to reach the executor within the plant In many cases the line of command was bypassed, i.e. orders were issued without the knowledge of immediate supervisors. Accordingly, Kuteyshchikov and his colleagues concluded that production and administrative discipline at the plant was weak.

A questionnaire was distributed among employees to find out what they knew about their rights and responsibilities. Every administrator was to indicate his idea of the management structure at the plant, his supervisor, his own rights and responsibilities, people authorized to put demands on him, the kind of these demands and, finally, the range of demands he can put on his subordinates.

Some employees turned out to have a rather inadequate concept of management structure as well of their rights and responsibilities. In a few cases an employee would think of a certain colleague as his supervisor – and vice versa. In most cases employees had no idea of their rights or responsibilities whatsoever.

The line of command was also ill-organized. Even simple matters required 3, 4 and more (up to 8!) authorizations that took from 2 to 7 working days to secure. On the other hand, senior management had to spend up to 70% of their time to address current issues that could easily be resolved by "low-level managers."[132]

The management system at the plant was naturally judged to be dismal. Yet upon making this conclusion TsIT orga-station employees proceeded with appropriate (and wise) caution. Rather than immediately revamping the entire system they opted for gradual reforms starting with a forceful introduction of new management discipline and a strict execution system that would be deeply rooted in every worker's mentality.

The orga-station made the following sound recommendations concerning early management reforms.

Senior management should strictly control their time. A list of managers should be drawn for scheduled meetings with the director (and his deputies) to discuss most important matters and current reports. Otherwise the director's office would be crowded, he would jump from one issue to another without a chance to

---

[132] Kuteyshchikov quotes comical examples when, say, the chief accountant was approached with regard to misplaced galoshes or a need to repaint a filing cabinet (Ibid, p.59).

carefully consider any of them. It is also critical that at least 15-20% of the working day be allocated to the administrator's personal business.

Orders should be written rather than verbal. Most orders are disregarded precisely because they are verbal and therefore can be easily forgotten by the manager and the subordinate whose fault is not always easy to ascertain.

The factory should have its own mail system.

A clear system of employees' responsibilities with stiff penalties should be introduced.

Only after every worker at the plant gets accustomed to these new rules, Kuteyshchikov maintained, one can move to a fundamental restructuring of the old system. Moreover, he believed that the implementation of these preliminary measures provided valuable data for elaborating new administrative arrangements.[133] As we see, the "narrow base" methodology plays a key role in this approach.

Some of the pilot stations were converted to so called orgbureaus, practical innovation departments established by the enterprise (institution) itself. Orgbureaus came to be even more popular than orga-stations since they focused exclusively on practical innovation for the given enterprise.

The third period in the history of in-house practical innovation departments (PID) started in 1925 when the First All-Union Conference on Practical Innovation acknowledged such organizations as the best tool for improving management. After a period of rapid growth PIDs became an integral part of enterprises and institutions.

---

[133] Ibid. P. 61.

These departments certainly faced numerous problems such as the lack of financing, the (understandable) scarcity of professionals and the occasional misinterpretation of their functions by senior management. On the whole, however, establishing PIDs from the bottom to the very top of the economy, i.e. at factories, trusts, ministerial departments and the Ministry of Economy, was a sound idea.

Numerous government documents, particularly an order from the Ministry of Economy dated October 17, 1928 determined that senior managers at all levels were responsible for practical innovation efforts/ "Any other approach would have been a disaster."[134]

Consultations and practical innovation efforts by about 2,000 TsIT pilot stations and orga-stations at Russian enterprises yielded tangible results. TsIT's popularity among industrial managers was growing fast. The institute was approached by numerous new customers seeking improvements in production and management. By the fall of 1923 the number of requests submitted to TsIT had increased so much that Gastev started thinking about setting up a new agency (a special joint-stock company) to deal with consultations and practical innovation. On July 8, 1924 the Council for Labor and Defense approved the charter of the *Setup* self-financing trust under TsIT. In those times it was a unique institutional arrangement.

Under p. 1 of the Charter, the trust was established "to provide consultations to the industry, retail companies and government agencies concerning management systems and their restructuring to improve economic efficiency and the use of workforce; to implement such reorganization of enterprises and agencies with the said objective; to improve work skills of employees using the work setup method developed by the Central Institute of Labor."[135]

---

[134] "Za ratsionalizatsyu" *[For Practical Innovation],* 1928, No.8, P. 11-12.

This TsIT affiliate focused primarily on practical innovation, applying the principles of NOT to improve labor, production and management. It goes without saying that the trust (much like individual orga-stations) was also doing some theoretical work of national significance rather that just taking advantage of ready-made theories available from TsIT.

The new trust was an efficient proposition. As early as by April 1, 1925 it happened to generate enough profit to replace TsIT's government financing. As an intermediary between the institute and the industry, the Setup trust (along with orga-stations) engaged in scientific management and professional training on an incredible scale. Its experience is still of interest today. TsIT's methodology was used to reorganize hundreds of enterprises and agencies, with savings coming to millions of rubles.

Last but not least, TsIT had another institutional arrangement for practical innovation that was its favorite. The institute dispatched *special instructors* to develop restructuring projects, review existing processes, implement new systems and help with their launch and operation. Gastev believed that guidance was *"our main leverage."* Vizgalin, his colleague from TsIT, wrote that consultations as such (in the narrow sense of the word) are little more than "a good wish that is never binding for anybody." One can compile volumes of research papers and suggest unquestionable reforms of work methods yet all the advice would stay on paper without people who are capable of applying these recommendations in real life. "Though local workers often know about the flaws in their management system and ways to fix them, the situation hardly changes and the system remains inadequate."[136]

---

[135] V. Pertsov. *TsIT's evolution and the Setup Joint-Stock Company [Evoliutsyya TsITa i Aktsionernoe o-vo Ustanovka]*. Organizatsiya truda [Labor Management], 1924, No.8-9, p.15.

[136] A.Vizgalin, *Basic trends in TsIT consultation work* [Osnovnye tendentsii konsultatsionnoi raboty TsITa.] "Organizatsiya truda", 1924, No.6-7, p.23.

Vizgalin reasonably notes that even a brilliant consultation approved at every level of management may prove utterly fruitless, and endorses TsIT's slogan: "From consultations to practical guidance!" With this approach "we do more than just planning, we are in charge of implementation; a plan can be challenged but a system in place cannot."[137]

Practical guidance provided by TsIT consultants was of course based on the **setup methodology,** the core of vocational training and a source of the **setup method for corporate restructuring.** Gastev's school believed that any new system should be introduced in a careful and gradual way rather than by force.

According to Gastev, practical guidance, while helping enterprises reach their economic goals, "stimulates incessant creativity in working masses. A consultant using [TsIT – *author's note*] methodology at a given factory, tomorrow would become an organizer of a new production unit, a bearer of new production culture in new regions."

TsIT's management consultants, with this broad spectrum of institutional arrangements, did not have an easy life. They had to fight age-old traditions and routines. Gastev openly claimed that this "reinforced concrete" conservatism and these "routine social instincts" were typical not only of administrators or small business owners, but also of "today's working class." Do not think, he wrote, that "a good project approved by somebody, endorsed by scientists and even a number of practitioners would for this sole reason easily overcome the inherent resistance of the live industrial crowd at the enterprise, from the director to the greaser."[138]

These "routine social instincts" could defeat even "the most outstanding" innovator.. For instance, Taylor, who "was putting

---

[137] Ibid.
[138] A.K. Gastev, *Production Setup Using TsIT Methodology* [Ustanovka proizvodstva metodom TsIT]. Moscow, 1925, pp. 8-9.

heroic pressure on the routine", occasionally had "to flee the factory" chased both by workers "who thought he was after heavier exploitation and by short-sighted managers who had no trust in his system."[139] Taylor worked in a much more favorable technological, economic, social and political environment that the Russian NOT pioneers in the 20s. Rank-and-file, "everyday" innovators were facing an even greater resistance, especially because their ranks included "an army of ungifted students" who substituted "working groups and meetings" for creative research, therefore adding to existing prejudices against innovation.

A workman with a supervisor holding a stopwatch behind his back, Gastev noted, would understandably be reluctant to change. This resistance was a natural" defense instinct" against intrusion into their work that could ostensibly drive down wages and increase the workload. Gastev had enough courage to claim that this internal resistance was not inherent to capitalism only. «This would be a blatant lie. Here, in Soviet Russia, we also see thousands of cases when workers instinctively protest against being monitored and even challenge any research into their work process."[140]

A still fiercer resistance often came from factory management (directors, engineers, foremen and so on) who thought that new organization technologies infringe on their "personal freedom to act." Practical innovation in Soviet Russia, wrote Gastev, becomes many times as challenging because every step must be discussed with "somebody". The innovator is never independent; he "must deal with a score or two of meetings where everyone jumps at a chance to share his bewilderment, occasionally his knowledge and most often … just his sheer stupidity somewhat embellished with eloquence (these days we all know how to be an orator)."[141]

---

[139] Ibid, p. 9.
[140] Ibid. P. 11.

He further notes that this massive rock of conservatism, routine and (often fierce) resistance cannot be shattered without great willpower and "organizational heroism." Any corporate restructuring plan must therefore deal with "crushing this resistance." Government offers little if any help in this case, so "we should apply some *special method*" that would overrun resistance from employees, foster a constructive attitude and enjoy support from "the live productive masses." Such a method ("the setup methodology") along with the program of corporate and cultural transformation was indeed developed by TsIT under Gastev's guidance.

2. Setup methodology for enterprise restructuring.

In sharp contrast to systems developed by Taylor or Ford, as we have mentioned more than once, all TsIT practical innovation projects at enterprises and agencies focused on personnel retraining. The setup method of corporate restructuring (SMCR) developed by Gastev is a detailed eight-part program of "natural" reforms based on dramatically changing the workers. "Rather than launching major reforms, - Gastev wrote, - ... we start with cultivating the live workforce," i.e. conduct preliminary training, as a basis for "infiltrating the workshops and, at a later stage, the entire enterprise."[142] Let us discuss the components of Gastev's methodology at some length.

Section 1 describes the process of personnel training in new work setups, or, to use Gastev's own term, that of *retraining.* This preliminary work was done *outside* of the enterprise, either at TsIT itself (through appropriate courses attended by some the factory personnel after hours) or at a *special setup workshop* established near the factory.

---

[141] Ibid.
[142] Ibid, p.20.

Such retraining, according to Gastev, was aimed at "fostering efficient techniques, capacity for organization, analytical work skills, general alertness and innovation."

So what was taught at these setup workshops or at TsiT courses? First of all, the elements of *motion culture* "that would precisely determine all work motions and encourage psychological flexibility." Motion training took place in a "spotlessly clean" environment of impeccable order and strict discipline. The trainees were offered a special system of **work setup techniques** (developed by TsIT) with the use of *templates,* special tools providing "static setups that determine any motion"; *guides* to cultivate precise motions; and *drivers* to "forcefully generate motion instincts that would serve as permanent setups in future work."

After these elementary work techniques were learned and "became a work instinct," the students moved on to **operation training.** They used precise techniques to meet their task, passed a test for each technique and applied it at a calculated speed.

The TsIT system, as noted above, was complemented with special **psychological training** to aimed at cultivate the *power of precise observation and memorizing.*

Finally, the training process involved a **time self-study** where the worker recorded the time spent on a given operation on his instruction (control) card. This step, according to Gastev, was a means of self-control that "clearly testified to the success of retraining." "We endow the worker with new organizational and production vigor and believe that in the future such retraining should become **a permanent feature in industry** (the italics are mine – author)."[143]

---

[143] Ibid, p.24.

Section 2. After special training of select factory personnel at the in-house setup workshop (or at TsIT) Gastevites started "invading" factory work areas. At this point the personnel already trained would acquire "new dexterity and new refined techniques". No changes were made to manufacturing processes yet. The main objective was to make the premises *"**spotlessly clean and tidy**"*. Mere campaigning for cleanliness and order among workers would be Sisyphean labor, Gastev wrote. Campaigning alone simply "does not work" and routinely ends in some kind of "business meetings", "commissions" and so on. Hence "on a Sunday or after working hours we clean the workshop ourselves and bring it into perfect order, much like the plant's laundrywomen and janitors. We take care of everything including workplaces, the floor, machine tools and workbenches so that personnel reporting to work would take this tidiness for a fact... A worker facing this new uplifting atmosphere develops a habit of keeping things clean.'" This cultural setup was believed to be "the first step, the first introduction to streamlined work."[144]

Section 3. TsIT fellows and trained personnel deal with *"**finishing the workplace**".* This process entailed the establishment of precise setups such as *static setups* (selection of the most comfortable sitting or standing position for every worker), *dynamic setups* (mastering the most efficient motions), *sensory setups* (related to vision and hearing, e.g. the optimization of lighting) and so on. At this stage "workers who already went through preliminary training would develop a keener interest in the order imposed on their workplace... in tools, in small but conspicuous everyday instruments. At this stage *the creative devil* would already wake up in every man to make him refine his workplace where he spends one third of his life."[145]

Section 4. This stage involves the "invasion" of manufacturing processes per se. The shop manager gets a

---

[144] Ibid, p. 25.
[145] Ibid, p. 26.

permanent assistant (*operation setup officer)* whose duties include individual guidance and general fine-tuning. He first identifies the static factors of a given operation, and then its dynamic factors to analyze the *workflow* as precisely as possible.

The selection of operations for such analysis is critical, Gastev wrote. Repeated and/or typical operations should be given a priority over rare and exotic ones.

Once the workflow is described, Gastev recommended to master *operation precision* "by checking the efficiency of each technique and exercising strict quality control." Of equal significance is the next setup, namely *operation speed,* a key factor of productivity and labor intensity.

Operation productivity, according to Gastev, should be measured by means of *time self-studies,* whose results (the length of each operation and rest time) would be recorded on the *instruction card.*

Again, Gastev's methodology centers on the same "narrow base" idea that he always contrasted with the so called "comprehensive coverage". This concept has an excellent historical record. Taylor himself, Gastev wrote, "was crazy" with a single operation of cutting or even "skinning". Yet this obsession ultimately resulted in scientific management itself. Or consider Gantt's charts that first applied to individual factory shops and later to whole factories. During the war Gantt elaborated a chart to manage the nationwide manufacturing of arms and military supplies. Note also that revolutions in the military industry often start with refining a single operation and its implements and rapidly spread to numerous other operations. Studies on such a "narrow issue" as feeding material for industrial processing finally gave rise to a brand-new way of manufacturing so that the very words "conveyor system" sound like the essence of modern industry. "This is what meticulous work on a single operation can mean."

Gastev trusted that his idea of operation setups would also become "an organizational storm" that would spread to industry as a whole. "We stand for a careful setup of each operation to increase its speed and precision. We know that a persistent drive for making an operation as refined as possible is often rewarded by the victory of this operation across the entire industry."[146] The above TsIT setups as applied to a single operation (workflow, operation precision and operation speed) could "inflame" the worker and stir his creative enthusiasm about refining other operations. Of course, a sound remuneration system should also be in place. Every worker who acts as a true **setup specialist** rather than a simple executor should be promoted to a higher pay grade and receive a reasonable bonus (up to 20% of basic wages).

Section 5. At this stage restructuring goes further by means of a careful **selection of operation setup instructors**. "Based on the previous four stages, now we have to methodically polish the necessary personnel."

Gastev suggested a three-part training methodology for such instructors that would supervise a given group of operations.
1. Psychological training to foster the power of precise observation and memorizing as well as analytical and management skills.
2. Training in constructive thinking, i.e. learning how to select different operations united by a certain constructive principle. 3. Learning how to combine the structural theory of operations with time.

"All those who pass an exam in organizational skills and show some talent for engineering will be introduced to the theory, structure and the engineering characteristics of particular operations, - Gastev wrote. – They will be the plant's **true frontline activists** that will later cooperate with TsIT's experts."[147]

---

[146] Ibid, p. 29.
[147] Ibid, p. 35.

Section 6. The previous stages were aimed at fostering a certain culture of key work techniques and the art of carefully planning and performing an operation with the help of shop floor instructors, "the live leaders of certain operational setups." At the 6th stage Gastev recommends to start a critical job of establishing *a closed operational complex.* While admitting that nothing at a plant can be "closed", since all departments are more or less interdependent, he was talking about relatively closed operational complexes with *a steady supply of materials, uniform equipment* and a rather *distinct production cycle.* For instance, such operational complexes in machine shops would consist of lathes or milling machines that perform similar tasks. Assembly shops that need a comprehensive supply of parts and materials can even easier be divided into such closed complexes.

This stage implies a precise definition of *assembly operations, support needs* (in terms of personnel and equipment) and standard *schedules* that define the type of parts needed, the delivery time and supply "bottlenecks".

At the same stage Gastev recommended to establish a *spare parts supply scheme* that would include intermediate storage facilities as well as procedures for parts replacement and management.

Finally, the principal objective of the 6th stage is to develop *"standards for operational complexes* including the planning of individual operations as well as the organization of workflow for time and quality gains." A successful solution of this problem would be "a decisive victory and an important test."

Section 7. Gastev described this stage as "the deepest aspect of our invasion" that is crucial to "whether our fundamental restructuring is a success."[148] It *involves the recruitment of*

---

[148] Ibid, P. 40.

foremen and the works manager based on all the previous setups. These factory shop managers, Gastev wrote, would be responsible for *maintaining* the general workflow, general services and logistics. Their job description should clearly define their rights and responsibilities, in particular, ensuring the availability of parts and implements at all times, dealing with any "hindrances" and efficiently managing the workflow. Gastev wanted these people to be creative and down-to-earth, keen on "strict diagrams, precise calculations and balanced leadership."[149]

Section 8. *A dramatic restructuring of the entire factory* starts at this stage. **To** Gastev, any attempts to control the workflow without the previous seven stages were just "empty romantic planning". "We oppose static plans, dead and inflexible schemes," - he claimed. He believed that workflow restructuring is a *kinematic* rather than static process that requires *careful social engineering preparations*.

Accordingly, any industrial process reformer should:

1. Develop standards for operational complexes.
2. Set up a spare parts supply scheme, organize the work of support personnel and the operation of intermediate storage facilities to maintaining an appropriate level of supplies and ensure the timely delivery of parts.
3. Organize support staff ("live accumulators", i.e. warehouse managers, quality control staff, maintenance personnel and so on).
4. Set up a facility to manufacture the necessary tools and implements.

Gastev believed *speed* and *precision* to be the main efficiency criteria for the overall workflow. He suggests a list of the most valuable *acceleration* methods.

---

[149] Ibid.

1. The workflow must be continuous; any breaks between operations must be eliminated.

2. The product should be passed for the next operation as fast as possible.

3. The product should be passed to the next operation directly.

4. The workflow must be synchronized.

5. Operations should be consolidated.

6. Operations should be differentiated, i.e. one operation should be divided into several stages and the easier ones should be assigned to lower-skill workers.

7. Operations must be performed at a maximum capacity of a given machine or man.

8. Standards should be established for materials, tools and workforce.

9. The finished product must be collected and stored (*accumulated*).

Gastev also identifies the means of achieving **precision.**

1. Availability of a drawing or a draft.

2. Availability of measuring tools.

3. Availability of measuring rods (for mass operations).

4. Fast quality control.

5. Precise standards and allowances should be shown in drawings and control templates.

6. Quality control checks covering all products or a random sample, with certain bonus payments to first-stage quality control workers.

However, simply planning the general workflow is not enough, Gastev wrote. Care should be taken of *live creativity stimulators.* i.e. the training of skilled staff (setup experts, foremen, works managers, warehouse managers and so on).

One of Gastev's interesting ideas was to establish enterprise "setup bureaus" whose managers would act as special aides to the director. Such bureaus would perform the following functions:

A. Continuous personnel retraining (the biological setup function).;

B. Adjustment of implements for the workflow and individual operations (the organizational setup function);

C. Fostering cultural setups at the entire factory (the cultural setup function).

Not in a shy way, Gastev claimed that his methodology led to "a truly natural update of manufacturing processes" and described it as "genuine social engineering" "that will provide a final answer not to problems of machines and men but to those of machine-men, i.e. a certain complex of naturally merged machines and men."[150] He always insisted that man plays a leading role in this complex. Therefore, the overarching objective of his program was to "rework man as the main actor of work by fostering entirely new cultural reflexes and encouraging initiative."[151]

To sum up, Gastev's system as a whole (including the general theory, training and retraining methods and the methodology of enterprise restructuring) ought to be recognized as something highly original. ***This comprehensive system covered a variety of areas such as engineering, technology, biology, psychophysiology, economics, history and education. Moreover, it contained prototype elements of sciences like cybernetics, human engineering, ergonomics and praxeology that emerged in later years. No wonder Gastev called his system "a techno-bio-social concept."***

Most Russian management scholars at first almost hysterically rejected Gastev's system. Time has shown, however,

---

[150] Ibid, p. 45.
[151] Ibid.

that a concrete and sensible "narrow base" approach proved to be arguably the only trend in the country that was capable of long and productive development. **Gastev's philosophy** never got lost in general problems of NOT, neither did he seek to reach the abstract heights where the live colors of scientific management start fading. It did, however, provide a "narrow" course of work that led Gastev to a sound long-term success.

It was Gastev's focus on man (the human factor) that made his theory so distinct and attracted increasing attention to it in the West.

Indeed, massive unemployment along with a shortage of skilled labor prompted foreign scholars to appreciate the role of man as the principal driving force of manufacturing that cannot be replaced by any technological innovations. The deeper was this understanding, the greater popularity Gastev's ideas enjoyed across the industrialized world. Following Gastev, Western scholars turned to the issues of principal human faculties and their development. Of course, as noted by Ishlondsky, they had first to overcome the initial prejudices against TsIT's ideas and methods and realize that "something good can come from Nazareth..." However, "we see how arrogance and skepticism in the West give way to amazement and question marks, how this amazement transforms into recognition that gradually becomes outright rather than cautious, how this recognition triggers a growing interest and, finally, people start advocating pilot projects and a broad application of TsIT methods in the West, with its superior culture, greater energy and a more industrious workforce." [152] He further adds that the West expected even more from the "Russian experience" than claimed by TsIT itself.[153]

---

[152]Ishlondsky I.E. TsIT and foreign countries. *[TsIT i zagranitsa]*. "Organizatsiya truda", 1925, No.4-5. P. 63.
[153]Ibid.

Gastev's workforce training and enterprise restructuring methodologies as applied by TsIT were especially popular outside Russia. As Frank Gilbreth, a leading authority in scientific management, put it, Gastev's papers demonstrated that "the Russians have a deeper understanding of NOT than we do."[154] The First International NOT Congress (Prague, 1924) was particularly noteworthy in this regard. The Russian delegation included A. Gastev, N. Bernstein and A. Labutin (all from TsIT), E. Rozmirovich (People's Commissariat of Workers' and Peasants' Inspectorate), I. Shpilreyn (industrial psychotechnics laboratory under the People's Commissariat of Labor), M. Vasiliev (People's Commissariat of Transportation) and F.Noa (All-Russian Association of Engineers). Gastev made his presentation in French and Bernshteyn in English. The former dealt with TsIT's setup methodology, the latter with standardization of motions. Unlike other presentations, those by Gastev and Bernshteyn triggered a vivid discussion. TsIT's methodology generated so much interest that Gastev and his colleagues were immediately invited to implement it at a leading European factory where a special shop would be made available. "We are far from being deluded with our success, but in any event the Congress demonstrated that our work has come to stir international interest, as evidenced, in particular, by papers on our methodology that start appearing in Western Europe and America."[155] Indeed, **after the Prague congress Western scholars began exploiting and using "the Russian experience", a formidable success for Gastev and TsIT.**

Gastev and his brilliant team, therefore, should be credited with extraordinary achievements. We agree with A.I. Berg, member of the Soviet Academy of Sciences, who said that we could learn a lot from the creative legacy of this outstanding pioneer in scientific management.

---

[154]Ibid.
[155]"Organizatsiya truda", 1924, No.6-7. P. 68.

This certainly does not mean that TsIT retraining and enterprise restructuring methodologies were absolutely perfect.

First, Gastev and his colleagues *focused their training efforts on workers,* though often paying lip service to training "a highly skilled workforce." However, white-collar specialists, i.e. managers or "social engineers" accounted for a negligible fraction of this workforce, which seems quite natural in the light of Gastev's general philosophy. Indeed, he believed that management was not fundamentally different from manual labor, and a skilled lathe operator, metal worker or training instructor can easily manage a shop, a factory or even the state. Gastev did suspect that these ideas were somewhat on the primitive side; TsIT even had a training course for administrators whose curriculum, however, was too vague, while attempts to establish a Labor University to train business managers failed for the same lack of theoretical and strategic arguments.

Second, *it appears that Gastev overestimated the future impact of his theories,* occasionally even to the point of losing contact with reality. S.G. Strumilin at the First All-Russian NOT Conference said he "admired Gastev's unconventional mind even when he speaks in paradoxes."[156] In fact, the founder of TsIT was not entirely alien to fantasies. As a scholar, he apparently was under a strong influence of many years spent in France and the works of French socialist Utopians. These, as is well-known, maintained that a socialist system established on the initiative of small groups of zealots would dramatically increase labor efficiency, since these groups would convey their inspiration ("inoculate with the germ", to use Gastev's words) to the rest of society.

Gastev believed in the advantages of the new system that ostensibly created a fundamentally new social environment and a fundamentally new worker. The abolishment of private property and the liquidation of the notorious figure of the entrepreneur

---

[156]Proceedings of the First All-Russian Initiating NOT Conference. Vol. 6. P. 26.

were proclaimed to eliminate the basic antagonistic contradiction between labor and capital. The role of financial remuneration in this case was supposed to start falling to zero. Gastev, it seems, partially shared the well-known idea that man in the new society would have a new social mentality that would facilitate the learning of Gastev's concept ("the germ") and, in the long run, boost labor efficiency.

In reality the new system that ignored financial incentives, a key source of energy that made workers keenly interested in higher productivity, was killing any potential for economic progress. No scientific management, however advanced, could possibly replace this source of efficiency.

Note that even some of Gastev's contemporaries such as B.D. Brutskus had reasonable doubts about the feasibility of fostering a new worker's mentality. Drastic changes are hardly possible in this area, Brutskus wrote, since economic activities are guided by common egotistical factors rather than methodologies (unless, of course, humans "turn into angels").[157]

The scholar did not assert that social life is entirely pragmatic; however, altruism belongs to creative work, personal relations or the quest for eternal values rather than workplace. "You cannot expect people to bake bread, stitch jackboots or make clothing on a daily basis for free, or for the sake of some distant (and probably unknown) others rather than for their friends and family... Spinoza had a dire spiritual urge to write his treatises; he would still write them even under a threat of jail, but he certainly polished lenses for money." "Economic policies that disregard this provision of political economy deny the basic laws of human nature."[158]

---

[157]Brutskus B.D. The Socialist Economy. Theoretical thoughts on Russian experience. *[Sotsialisticheskoe khozyaystvo. Teoreticheskie mysli po povodu russkogo opyta]*. Paris, 1988. P. 63.
[158]Ibid. P. 74-75.

Unfortunately, this statement fully applies to the "work germ" concept developed by Gastev and his colleagues–though, to be fair, all "builders of the Communist society" were denying the same basic laws of human nature for many decades with an even greater enthusiasm.

All these comments notwithstanding, let us once again TsIT's methodology was used to train hundreds of thousands of workers, tens of thousands of shop floor instructors, and brought millions of rubles in savings from practical innovation and restructuring.

To sum up, Gastev's system was so different from its Western counterparts primarily because it naturally incorporated research, training and practical innovation efforts to produce a unique, or, rather, "triune" mechanism for scientific management.

PART II. A.K. Gastev's selected works.

1. New cultural setup.[159]

---

[159] Reprinted with minimal abridgements from *A. Gastev. New cultural setup*

The issue of culture is now central to the USSR. It is discussed in a multitude of papers, books, letters and articles. However, all these discussions are blatantly ideological. They pay scant attention to the true economic foundation for building the culture everyone is talking about.

Constructive discussions on culture must be based on the static and dynamic elements of current reality. Otherwise they risk turning into a purely literary exercise that would soon wear out just like all those slogans of yesteryear calling, say, for propaganda of efficiency. Many people think that culture depends on scientific management (NOT). It is clear, however, that the general objective of NOT and its aims such as speed, time and standardization have only a formal link to culture. Such cultural deliberations would soon become void if they do not rest on resolute economic policies. To unite masses, formal slogans should be forged rather than merely proclaimed. Even the slogan of religion spread among broad masses only with the advent of an appropriate economic environment. Any serious attitude to culture should rely upon **fundamental economic trends** that spontaneously help reach cultural objectives. Such trends should be identified, described and conveniently systematized.

1.Economic recovery.

Let us start with noting that the first fierce stage of the revolutionary storm and stress is now over. Any new revolutionary movement, if it transpires, would obviously either be more broad-based than now or would be very different from the previous phases.

The current era is primarily that of peaceful *economic development,* as clearly illustrated by just one economic slogan of restoring the pre-war level of production. The robust economic

---

[Novaya kulturnaya ustanovka], Moscow,1923.

activity in the country is aimed at reaching prosperity in the USSR. Indeed, we can now talk about *economic recovery.*

This recovery has clearly had an impact on our highest government authority, the People's Commissariat of Finance. The managing function and the economic role of public finance have not been appreciated enough. Financial agencies, including PCF, are viewed in terms of fiscal matters or subsidies. In reality, however, PCF, much like its counterparts in capitalist Western Europe such as ministries of finance and banks, acts as a brisk *manager and the leaven* of economic life. In its impressive recent experiments PCF has reduced currency issue, introduced bank money, established a budget control system for government agencies, stabilized the ruble and drafted the annual budget. All this demonstrates that namely PCF is the true manager of the country, a powerful economic leaven. As such, it should be credited with restricting our anarchic willpower to certain financial boundaries, as well as with teaching us economic dexterity and prudence. No need to say that PCF also organizes our entire life. This conscious conductor of our economic policy is *forcing everyone to catch up,* fix walkways, streets and roads; deftly organize storage of goods; control traffic and so on. Opinions on its economic policy may of course vary. Many government agencies may be cursing PCF for drastic budget cuts. In any event, however, PCF is a graphic example of a good way to manage the economy. It has certainly restored Russian finances. It pays more attention than anybody to revolutionary economic innovation and initiative.

More evidence on economic initiatives may be found in *large and small projects* launched by various government agencies, occasionally in smart cooperation with foreign, cooperative, peasant and private capital. Heroic examples of economic management are growing in number before our very eyes, and so do examples of personal and collective economic victories. We shall not dwell upon these particular indicators of a healthy economy in more detail. We shall just say that no culture can be developed without due regard to these grandiose movements and the signs of a true economic recovery in the country.

2. Sources of culture

In its tremendous effort to restore the economy Russia has set in motion a number of key mechanisms that emerged very recently. First and foremost, we mean *industry* that has stirred up our sleeping agrarian country, imparted a new speed to the entire economy, woke up vast slumbering wastelands and given rise to a new type of labor management. Industry, whether private or state-owned, has been highly instrumental to the new culture meant to stop Russia's stagnation. Accurate processing, precise motions and fast delivery – all these were given to us by industry.

Another major factor of culture was *the world war* that plunged millions of people into a psychologically tense atmosphere, made them appreciate time, taught them how to act at the brink of death and dealt a heavy blow to Russian sluggishness. The world war with its horror, death and ashes, arguably triggered the popular revolt in Russia that led the country to its present life and its emerging new culture.

Revolutions, especially our October revolution, should be seen as a new source of culture that sends a new message to the masses and relies on anonymous people, social creativity and initiative. At the same time the revolution has set an objective of keeping up with the slogans written on its banner in all its economic achievements. We mean the slogans of a *socialist state* that grants equal rights to all citizens, especially the so called "low classes", i.e. workers and peasants.

Revolution has also turned the government into an unprecedented regulator and manager of social life, as well as the supreme creator of culture. While in old days the government also was in charge of enormous facilities such as railways and military plants, it never played such a leading social and economic role as it does now. Our culture, therefore, must be the culture of governance as well.

Finally, do not forget the last source of culture, that is, the unique agrarian nature of our country. Russia carried out a major revolution thanks to its workers and peasants but now, as the peasant character of the country has become so evident, its links to the above-mentioned sources must be taken into account,

3. Types of economic art

The current Soviet economy features the types of economic art (sectors) such the government-regulated sector, the state-owned sector, the independent initiatives of certain government agents and enterprises, the cooperative sector, the private sector (somewhat regulated or supervised by the government) and, finally, large farms that can span almost twenty kilometers.

This huge economic system as a whole was hardly borrowed from America. While in the past its management was based on incredible resourcefulness, today we associate it with speed and precision. These special methods of economic management are hardly a copy of the capitalist initiative.

Our economic art is *far more sophisticated.* We need to be accurate, ingenious and fast. At the same time we need to profess statism with a certain social bias. Our economic recovery is clearly a greater challenge than anything in the US. Let us discuss individual types of economic art in greater detail. The public sector in old Russia was managed in a routine way. It was following an established path according to a calculated long-term program. In contrast, today's public sector heavily depends on maneuvering. This equally applies to enterprises producing goods for the so called private market and even military factories that have to be on the alert at all times to meet new demands. Today's economic initiative by public servants has no precedents in Western Europe. Our "red director" can be chairman or a member of the board of some trust, he can organize some new economic committee. He is a government agent, a sworn public servant who must follow instructions from the government. At the same time he must be a highly resourceful person to deal with daily challenges, wriggle out of difficult situations and sometimes doing things from scratch on his own initiative. Many a man cannot survive in such an overheated atmosphere.

Many others settle down as rotten bureaucrats or become adventurists. Yet we do have this special type of a manager who can combine public service with enormous personal initiative (1).

Our cooperative sector also does not fit the European or American framework. This sector must be thrifty with scarce raw materials and foreign exchange while adapting to the changing needs of the peasant masses. In short, it operates in a far less idyllic environment than cooperators in Western Europe. Recalling that the cooperative sector also addresses government needs and acts as a bridge between the public sector and the private sector, one can imagine the kind of strategic talents needed from the manager of a cooperative. At the same time Russia still has an immense population of peasants who in fact lean towards the capitalist system. Conscious and active rural individuals or groups capable of working on government tasks are still rare.

All these types of economic art are ultimately responsible for defining the culture we have to struggle for. This culture, paradoxically, will have no precedent in bourgeois cultures and, most likely, will not directly borrow from the ideology of the future.

4. Electrification as a path to culture

Electrification enjoys well-deserved yet rather formal fame in Russia. Few books have been written on this subject, and its specific details are hardly known to the general public. Yet the master plan for electrification has in fact outlined the principal development paths for our culture.

Electrification is a huge machine that is being built on an agrarian parade ground and wasteland called Russia. Its electric paws reach beyond the traditional cultural center of the country. The map of electrification shows new areas of cultural progress and industrial development in post-revolutionary Russia. Its long paws extend from the center to the east, south-east, Turkestan. The Volga, the Russian North and Siberia.

Once a certain supply of electric power is secured for central Russia, the plan is to gradually move to remote areas. Moreover, it implies a gradual resettlement of our entire culture from St. Petersburg and the Moscow area to the east, particularly the Volga region whose development has just started. Also, under the master plan the existing railways will be electrified and new tracks, electrified as well as regular, will be laid in the South-East, Turkestan, the North and Siberia

A careful look into this plan and a number of underlying economic and engineering studies (such as Prof. Grinevetsky's "Post-war prospects for the Russian Industry") would show that the plan of electrification essentially means *a **revolutionary colonization of the country.***

After the separation of Poland, the loss of communication with Finland and a severe economic blow suffered by Petrograd is was only natural to turn our economic eye to the East. This need for the revolutionary colonization of Russia has already brought about large agencies such as Severoles, Sibles, the Nizhny Novogorod Fair Committee, the Siberian Railway Committee in Irbit and so on. The somewhat notorious word "colonization" has already gained currency. It is not necessarily carried out by a special agency; for instance, the Murmansk railway authority has its own colonization department.

Electrification plans mean a degree of industrialization combined with the development of large virgin lands. The main sign of this drive is the powerful move to the East. No wonder that the most exciting economic initiatives and the greatest economic flexibility prevail exactly in those economic sectors that deal with this process. We are obviously on the eve of some major changes associated with the move to the East.

The master plan of electrification will certainly be reviewed several times. Nevertheless, it still illustrates this move of our economy and, therefore, a shift in our general culture.

5.Energy of the people

Obsolete ideology still lingers, however. It will drag on for a long time. It centers on the attitude best expressed by Chekhov as "To Moscow! Let's go to Moscow!"
We badly need a very different slogan. Culture must spread. Instead of fleeing to Moscow, where peasant petitioners come to meet "Kalinin himself", where brilliant students live, where strings can be pulled at government agencies and wealthy speculators abound, we should foster a true popular, economic and cultural movement to the unfamiliar depths of the Russian hinterland.

"To virgin lands!" rather than "To Moscow!" would be a more appropriate slogan.

It would indeed support the emerging economic recovery, the implementation of economic plans and the ensuing cultural development could indeed be supported by a slogan "Go deeper!" Create culture on the spot. Do not move to the center, do not stick to the past by developing a bureaucratic culture. Do whatever you dream of right where you are now, with the limited available funds. Our new revolutionary society has largely inherited a custom of begging the government for money and privileges, as Russian merchants and petty bourgeoisie used to do. We should encourage a different slogan, that is, "Fight the routine!" If you feel unhappy with your situation, grab whatever instruments available and move to a new place. Just do not dream of "Moscow", the old comfortable center where you want to meet people who can pay you a subsidy. Likewise, do not dream of university enrollment. Metropolitan universities are bursting under the pressure of new students. They can accommodate fewer and fewer people. And even if the number of students doubles, these universities would be unlikely to foster a culture that the new vibrant Russian economy needs. We need local grassroots managers who would be loyal to the government yet resourceful and full of initiative.

Americanism, a popular topic in today's discussions, means restless energy rather than a fancy degree. All great American inventors and businessmen had no university degrees or sometimes even a high-school diploma. They were people of natural talents and energy who could come up with an invention in an abandoned railway car or a shack – and win. The man of culture whom we have to create in order to respond to economic recovery will obviously be very different from the well-read but sloppy members of the old Russian intelligentsia.

6. Creation of new cultural setups.

To win at the economic front with the pathetic fixed assets available, to forge economic flexibility and still be loyal to the government one needs certain special qualities that so far have remained fairly obscure. One can see traces of these qualities scattered over a variety of organizations. Sometimes it's just a hint, sometimes an isolated policy. All these signs have to synthesized. This cultural setup must be designed to ideally fit the future economy. We need this type of people. We need a culture of dexterity.

The very culture as we understand it is nothing else but technological and social dexterity. Such a culture requires a number of qualities we shall call setups. Cultural setups are biological and social qualities that guarantee a cultural and social victory to their bearer. A list of such qualities can obviously be drawn from the above-mentioned sources and from the objectives set by our plans of economic development.

7. Cultural setup program

Below we shall analyze the various elements of our program that we would like to regard as a methodology. Once the movement for this program takes final shape, we should be able to make it more specific. What follows at this point is just a conceptual review.

A. OBSERVATION POWER

The improvement of human senses, particularly vision and hearing, is on the top of our agenda. Keen vision and hearing, maybe aided with some special devices, is a means of fostering *focused attention.*

The capacity for focusing one's attention at any time and at any object, for limiting this object to a certain area or a certain motion should be viewed as the ABC of this new cultural setup. This implies *alertness* as a quality inherent to any good observer. The cultural man we need can listen, understand, switch from his current business to another activity (which may be entirely different) at any moment. Observation techniques ought to be studied by a special science, researched and described in practical manuals. We believe that observation power is a step to *life analysis.* Reality can be analyzed in earnest only by a person who is used to accurate observation, can concentrate fast and can separate an object or a process he observes into individual interrelated elements.

106

Modern schools can hardly teach observation power. Despite all reforms, they rather encourage careful self-observation and superficial setups. In the meantime, observation power has become a matter of considerable attention outside Russia as well. Some teaching trends in Western Europe (like Montessori's lab method) are based on observation power training. They are dwarfed, however, by the broad scope of boy scouting, a movement that largely emerged as a *reaction to inadequate high school education.*

We need not talk here about the specific bourgeois features of boy scouting (such as intelligence gathering in wars against indigenous colonial nations). We shall just note that modern cultural nations that generally employ a special "greenhouse" way of observation and thinking have decided to teach a primitive, almost savage observation power to their young generation. We have to admit that good skills at using observation tools such as a compass, a watch, a chronometer, binoculars or a spyglass, as well as orientation skills in an urban or wild environment are indispensable to our new cultural setup. Observation power indicators may range from simple to highly sophisticated ones, so training may start with a skill to determine the time of day from the position of the sun or the movement of people in the streets to the ability to handle delicate chronoscopic instruments. In any event, special training in observation power, be it through school exercises, games played by young adults or special economic maneuvering must be thought of as *the basic quality* of the new cultural man. It should be opposed to ignorance, nonchalance and our Russian philosophical nihilism that shuns all "petty" and concrete things.

Observation power is the first school of analysis, initiative and victory.

B. CAPACITY FOR EXPRESSION

Observation power automatically generates a need to accurately express things (portray, reflect and record). Let us focus on *the word.* The tough and unambiguous language of business letters, the language of telegrams, a dialogue between businessmen at a bank or a railway station, exchanges between conductors of a departing train – in short, all the words that are born in a situation where time and space are at a premium, must be learned by the public for daily use. Words must be short, precise and clear-cut. Maybe even the experience of our newspaper reporters will not be sufficient to establish the necessary way of expression. Concise reporting as opposed to sophisticated discussions must become a weapon for our cultural setup workers.

The same applies to *writing.* For want of a luxury such as the art of shorthand mastered by every clerk or activist, we should at least expect any man of culture to use clear handwriting and a concise style, while writing at a speed of up to 3o words a minute. Learning shorthand would be the next step. It seems possible that exercises in writing speed and the use of concise language would be a far better way of training than composing wordy historical essays or works of literature. The very method of verbal and written expression must be spiced with precise measurements. The incoherent and confused folk speak whose metaphors and images are still officially praised should be discarded.

Everything should be measured in terms of time or space. All notes we give to various people should contain figures plus a short and precise text. A feeling of time or space limits should be an objective of our cultural education. Lofty literature as the focus of modern high school learning must be mercilessly replaced with the drawing, the draft and the graph. The art of *graphic representations,* all those abscissas and ordinates, has been limited to universities so far. We must abruptly and bluntly introduce it in lower schools to benefit any lathe operator or foundry man. All the equipment you need for that is probably just a grid paper notebook and a pencil, a fabulous assistant always available anywhere. They would keep reminding us that everything should be drawn and measured in exact figures.

An inexpensive yet smartly designed kit would come in handy to anybody person who wants to express what he observes by making sketches or precise drawings. Everybody must also *master the art of photography* in the literal sense of the word.

Only when you get used to a photo camera and appreciate the unquestionable evidence provided by the negative and the print as opposed to vague deliberations, you would fully understand the value of recording facts. Observation power supplemented with expression skills is the chief tool of the new cultural man.

B. WILLPOWER.

Training in observation power and expression skills already teaches us to be pragmatic and learn how to acquire an object. When we acquire an object we take it. Taking an object means being able to manage it and foster a special efficient prerequisite for work. Efficiency, capacity for acquisition, *preparedness for resolute action,* that is, willpower, must be recognized as a necessary feature of the new culture.

Fast response and *an easy transition from one act to another* typical of airplane pilots, drivers and other people who control their motions, are the features you need to forge willpower. Willpower means a capacity for immediate action and that for resolute systematic action. Persistent and even routine adherence to a once chosen path is the only key to victory. Willower is victory. A person who is set for relying on willpower is already a winner. He cannot have any fantasies, because he translates his ability to work into immediate action. Willpower is a decision that directly translates into action without any delay.

Fostering willpower in a modern man is needed as a breath of life. Whatever cultural qualities we might have, in the absence of willpower and tenacity we would be nothing but garbage. Willpower exercises must start in early childhood. Even pre-school children must learn to be resolute and stubborn. Willpower tests must be the most important tests at high school.

D. MOTION CULTURE

Motion culture as we understand it implies that we should literally move. It must be accepted as a reaction to modern frozen intellectual culture. *Man must move his own body* in acts such as attacking, counterattacking or chasing. His motions should be powerful, fast and accurate. Learning this art would create a new man with a new motion culture. Physical exercise is crucial to this process. It should become the most important custom of the new man with the new cultural setup. He would exercise in the morning to get a boost for the day. He would exercise in the evening to calm down and feel physically comfortable. Physical exercise also teaches man how to be brave, resolute, how to breathe with ease and always be ready for real action. This is the general objective of motion culture. In particular, it should also focus on cultivating the so called **work motions.**

A deft and well-aimed strike, a calculated amount of pressure applied for a precise period of time, artful handling of heavy objects must be appreciated as much as the greatest intellectual achievements.

E. DAILY ROUTINE

Motion culture needs a certain calculated order. A man who knows how to move or strike should follow a daily routine as the principal time management tool of the cultural setup.

We are talking about things that have been woefully neglected. The bed must be arranged for a good night sleep in any environment, be it in cultural Moscow or at the North Pole. A man must breathe fully and do breathing exercises several times a day. A man must chew properly so that food is half-digested in his mouth. A man must take care of his body, wash his face, massage and wipe the body, take a bath in any situation, be it in peaceful times or at a military camp.

Daily routine is clearly related to time management. Many think of it as a major loss of time. The opposite is in fact true: nothing saves you more time than daily discipline.

A time card with records made to within half an hour is a fast tool for learning the real daily routine. Such a card, made out of graph paper or even regular paper with a stenciled grid, is the main evidence of daily routine in action. While the card costs next no nothing, the daily routine actually *saves time wasted on extra sleep* as well as *meals* to produce a *surge of energy* and power in your body.

F. POLYTECHNISM

Our country is called a socialist republic. Our schools are called labor schools. Yet these schools provide insufficient general knowledge and inadequate labor skills. The issue of elementary labor polytechnism is no less crucial than that of following a daily routine. Fostering polytechnism in students is not an expensive proposition. Scores of plants are currently idle, while universities and high schools have numerous unused machines and tools. We propose the bare minimum that would still ensure a true introduction into labor practices. Training is needed in three areas: the techniques of using tools, the techniques of operating machines and assembly techniques.

Some techniques of using tools must be mastered with regard to dirt, wood and metal. Everyone should know the science of moving, striking and cutting these materials. Training in the use of simple implements such as the axe, the chisel, the hammer and the spade would make a person ready to go to any virgin land. Such training would truly introduce people to culture. A minimum of digging, a minimum of metal-working, a minimum of wood-working should be taught. That would be it. Serious vocational training should start with a test in the knowledge of these elementary work techniques.

Talking about *machines,* we mean those that are available anywhere, in cultural centers as well as in run-down small towns. Take a common drilling machine. You should earn how to turn the motor on and off, change speeds and do the drilling; if you make progress and want to learn other machine operations, take that same drilling machine and replace the drill on its spindle with a tapping tool, a miller and finally a cutter. Apart from drilling, your machine will be able to do milling, threading, planing or work as a lathe. It will be a truly universal introduction to the world of machines.

Let us move on to *assembly.*

We have to master the art of construction from simple pieces of wood and learn how to fasten them using grooves, bolts, nuts, staples and clamps. Finally, we need to learn how to adjust the assembly on the spot.

A person who has mastered the use of tools (including simple implements, machines and assembly tools) will not be afraid to go with a small tool kit to any place, from a modern factory to a wild forest. Moreover, he will never look at rails, machines and wheels at a machine-shop as a savage; he will "acquire" them and learn how to use them. His eyes will be intelligent and attentive, his attitude creative and efficient.

G. ORGANIZATION

The literary noise that has been made around the issue of scientific organization of work (NOT) often makes it difficult to seriously discuss organizational problems. We tend to start forgetting that organization was an objective of the human race ever since it appeared on Earth. Scientific management or NOT is evidence-based organization. An artful organizer or manager is a person who can do a job *under pressure,* i.e. when time or space are limited and the supply of tools or materials is scarce. He often has to sacrifice time for the sake of space and vice versa.

If tools are in short supply, he has to look for alternative materials. If materials are in short supply, he has to switch to other tools.

Accordingly, these four variables, i.e. time, space, tools and materials have to be flexible. Anyone who obscures this problem with fancy words such as normalization, organization and the like is a fake NOT expert rather than a business-like person. Real scientific management starts only after man is constrained and has to maneuver. Scientific management is not an abstract theory, a work of literature or a compilation. It inevitably comes to us and always rises from ashes. It would be a fallacy to think that NOT is possible only in America or at an industrial plant. It can be used anywhere in the Russian hinterland, in any peasant hut and on any road.

H. ECONOMIC RESOURCEFULLNESS

We have already noted that *maneuvering* has been a salient feature of economic initiatives and economic art in Russia. We always operate on a tight schedule; we are limited by decrees and the lack of capital. While PCF is shelling us with various orders on a daily basis, we also have to respond to surprise changes in market demand.   In this situation we have to foster special economic resourcefulness, that is, a capacity for fast maneuvering, first on a small and then on a broader scale. We are opposed to patronage and economic subsidies. We advocate good accounting, our own cultural setup, the power of observation, resourcefulness, willpower, motion culture, routine daily discipline, polytechnism and business-like setups. All this will make us capable of coming up with rapid and unexpected initiatives. We need to learn how to trade goods, buy things before the market goes into panic and precisely feel various economic fluctuations. One has to win in a situation where others are panicking, even at the expense of a temporary downturn in output. Resourcefulness and self-sufficiency without ever resorting to patrons are the qualities that distinguish a strong-minded manager from sleepyheads and daydreamers.

I. SOCIAL SETUPS

The previous setups largely referred to biology and management. Let us now turn to social setups. Economic maneuvering concerns things rather than people. However, people should be handled in the same way. First of all, the social setup must be based on charisma and certain affability (however artificial) instead of outright rudeness. Such qualities are inherent to any cultured nation. Also, we would like to shatter one old Russian prejudice. We are always expected to be sincere. We would suggest a different slogan. Sincerity is something akin to a child, a savage and a cultured European during a fierce battle. Cultured life, however, does not need this unnatural sincerity. It needs, if I may, certain cultural conventions that soften our everyday life and should be seen as a human right to be enjoyed in relations with others.

Teamwork is also an art. We are far from professing primitive everyday communism. It is good for nothing. Teamwork is an *art of kindling enthusiasm for particular work.* This requires obedience, enthusiastic management and iron will. Mere intellectual planning without passion is no good. We must learn the art of firing enthusiasm.

This applies to the art of management as well. Maybe managers do not need that much enthusiasm in our environment but in any event they must learn how to *give orders.*

Whereas "governance" usually means careful and calculated planning, the manager often has to act on the spur of the moment. He should end his maneuver when needed and never lose his spirits in new situations. He should also learn how to communicate with the masses of varying cultural background and lead these masses. This can be achieved only by means of special exercises and life experience.

Social setups also include the creation of *social capital.*

As already noted, government leadership must come hand in hand with economic initiative. This implies a certain structure of capital. If we set up a common business (even with little direct interference from the government) we have to address two issues from the outset. On the one hand, any business involves personal work or management activity; on the other hand, the fruit of this work should be pooled into a common pot. We need to establish a tradition of creating common social capital that would be less flexible and less "business-oriented" as its non-socialist counterpart. This social capital would largely correspond to fixed capital, while funds for maneuvering could therefore be called the working capital. Any establishment, from a huge plant to a tiny student credit union must set up the so called social capital.

All the qualities described above need to be developed once and for all. Observation power, resourcefulness, willpower, daily routine, work and organization are gradually becoming social setups. They are transforming from personal qualities and exercises into collective qualities and exercises. Therefore, combined with special training in personal influence, with a developed methodology of collective work and with social capital they would produce a true social cultural setup.

8. New agents of culture

A once coined aphorism claiming that the French in 1871 were defeated by the German schoolteacher still carries enormous weight in the world. People overwhelmingly believe that the so called public education can be a major independent factor of culture, the national or social victory of a given country. It should be evident from the above chapters that today's schools with their routine, inflexibility and unfit human material can hardly be called a factor of culture. We hold that true agents of new culture should come up from those *fast operators* of enterprises and agencies who possess the qualities discussed earlier. Military intelligence officers with their refined observation power, their ability to register and their wonderful life experience where time had to be measured to within a second must be thought of as agents of culture and praised as never before. Field engineers and military technicians who had used precise assembly instruction cards long before Taylor should also be included in the ranks of those creating a new culture. The Young Pioneers' organization has translated the best stories of adventure and victory into life, making a breakthrough towards new reality much more efficiently than any high school. A traffic policeman with his baton orchestrates pedestrian, horse and motor traffic – and teaches newcomers from the country how to move properly with an urban gait – is an excellent manager as well as a guide. Firemen who struggle with inventing a harness that can be put on a horse in 30 seconds are real agents of the new life that we are in need of. All of them are people of motion culture, signal and rapid will-driven action. Criminal investigators who gradually accumulate an inexhaustible wealth of observations, comparisons, combinations and analytical conclusions are better experts on psychology of the crowd and the individual than law school graduates or psychology lab technicians. Likewise, a newspaper reporter who never uses too many words, who registers events instantly and arrives at the incident scene fast is also a person who forms the new ranks of culture. Industrial time study experts who take every minute into account and conduct mass experiments involving rapid calculations and comparisons should also be taken into account as members of the emerging new movement for a new cultural setup.

Since we have just mentioned factories, let us recall a wonderful industrial institution of "service technicians" (or "adjusters" and "outfitters"). No literature is available about these amazing machine-tool professionals. Namely these technicians promote organization in industry. It was with their help that enterprises such as Putilovsky metal works managed to increase their employment from 10,000 in peace time to 50,000 during the war. A service technician's work can introduce manufacturing to the unskilled masses who have been too carefree to learn anything about the world. Take chief engineers who are responsible for the courageous deployment of new manufacturing processes and production control; take the senior technician who knows how to take care of machine-tools and other equipment – all these people contribute to the cultural setup that we need. Electricians and telephone linemen who are accustomed to exploring enormous spaces to lay wires fast and install insulation; technicians on duty at power stations who rivet all their attention to distribution switchboards are wonderful observers and excellent guards of the emerging culture. Chiefs of major railway junctions are ready to accommodate or dispatch loaded trains, find their way in mazes of tracks, draft and implement sophisticated schedules. This is where abscissas and ordinates should be learned. Builders of power stations or railway tracks provide examples of resourcefulness, the art of managing people and development skills. Assembly supervisors, foremen in charge of laying track or handling large machines are real experts who can teach us a lot. Heads of prospecting and research expeditions can teach us how to bring culture to remote areas, how to build a workers' town, a plant or a station in a godforsaken place in a few weeks' time. Throngs of clerks and agents at warehouses, offices, banks, information desks, countless shop assistants deftly handling goods in tight spaces teach us organization, dexterity and efficient processing. Finally, airplane pilots and truck drivers know how to rapidly change their psychological and motion setup. In a matter of seconds they would switch from the steering wheel to the brake, from changing the speed to gas feed, from a smooth motion to alarm. This is where live rather than dead psychology can be found. A surgeon who diagnoses a patient and immediately applies a knife, an orthopedist who actually reassembles a man and gives him an opportunity to move - these are the ranks of determined people who can teach us the synthetic culture that we need.

The scattered world of astute observers, masters of precise expression, adherents of strict daily routine, field service technicians, organizers and bearers of the new cultural setup is vast. We have mentioned just a few of its representatives as an illustration. Our main message is that modern schools, instead of relying heavily on ideology and stylized work training, must bring cultural education closer to actual current life.

9. High school routine

The modern school is primarily an ideological establishment. It certainly cannot cope with the pressure of the ambient real-life culture. It has no inherent ties with economic culture, its only savior. If we continue pursuing today's policies, even after years of hard work the community will be still maintaining but formal contacts with schools and view education as a matter of duty rather than training in management skills and initiative. Any modern school reforms (vocational training, laboratory teaching methods or links to agriculture) can by no means be productive unless supported by the mentality of those new people described above. Otherwise the school would be helpless and would teach, like its predecessor, nothing but basic literacy. Modern teachers may laugh when told that the best psychologists should be sought among police detectives, the best assembly men among field engineers and firemen, the best organizers among railway junction bosses, willpower teachers among surgeons and coaches and the best managers among foremen and apprentices. Despite the fact that we live in times when labor rules, our advice about school could seem extravagant. It is not only Russia, by the way, where teachers live on a pittance; in a civilized Western country such as France a rural schoolteacher has to moonlight as a shoe-maker.

The meager pay and striking boredom typical of modern high schools mean that only the least talented want to become teachers. Of course, as an exception, wonderfully gifted teachers and professors do exist. These, however, are rare heroes that serve their time in solitary cells of the large jail called school. The bulk of teachers are those no one has picked up for the needs of our initiative-based economy. Schools in fact attract losers who failed to master observation power, the art of expression, strong will, daily routine, true (rather than "greenhouse") polytechnism, fine organization, devilish ingenuity and the social setup.

It should obviously be *completely restructured* to be more than just a copy of best practices in Western Europe.

10. Grassroots movements

With further progress in economic initiatives in our country it will become even more evident that our schools can ill support economic development. No genius of a national leader and no loans would help here. What could help are the emerging grassroots movements based on exercise. Say, the Young Pioneers Organization was established as a reaction to stale school practices. Factory-based vocational schools, for all their drawbacks, are a reaction against high schools that mimic old-time classical schools, whatever new labor-oriented rhetoric they may use.

All the various clubs, athletic societies and leagues testify to the fact that high schools are incapable of forging efficiency, i.e. achieving their main objective. Schools just pay lip service to their official goals. We need to start a movement advocating economic initiative to foster the best citizens such as those discussed above. We need to establish special *economic initiative societies* as a key source of the new efficient culture. A dry official presentation on the organization of a fair in Nizhny Novgorod, a story of immense challenges faced by an expedition to Spitsbergen or a report by the captain of ship on a perilous voyage across the Kara Sea will be far more valuable than the scariest novel by Mayne Reid, and certainly do much more good than modern teaching methods in our schools.

Such stories would give rise to countless imitators, they would encourage persistent economic victories, they would gradually reshape schools and make them absorb all the organizational will that is inherent to economic development.

11. Rearing the young

Young people in Russia are making too much of slogans that they understand but formally, such as scientific management, time, speed, family and so on. No grassroots movement, however, can be based solely on ideology. Firstly, it must involve serious exercise that should be readily available to anyone in our democratic country. Secondly, it must be related to official economic and cultural efforts. Therefore, young people should establish corporations under the auspices of economic entities. The goal of such corporations would be to train people that strive for *economic victories* and know how to engage in risky economic maneuvering and meet the challenges of management.

Apart from abstract literature on management, the young generation should be familiar with some pages of our live history. Tell them the story of Ivan the Terrible who sent Stroganov to colonize Siberia. Recall Yermak, the famous explorer of unknown lands. Peter the Great, Catherine the Great, Count Potemkin, Demidov and others should exemplify the idea of colonization. Check our entire history. Recall that as early as under Catherine the Great a huge canal-digging project (as yet unfinished) was started in Siberia. Recall the impressive – and victorious – efforts on populating Siberia, remember all those Dutch, German, French, Bulgarian and Greek experts who helped the Russians develop god-forsaken places. Remember our remarkable self-taught engineers who managed to invent the best steam engines and other technologies simultaneously with their counterparts in Western Europe. Keep recalling our convicts, internal exiles and gold diggers who also acted as colonizers to bring culture to Siberia, the Russian North and the remote Turkestan.

A measure of patriotism would definitely not hurt here. Point to the Siberian railway that was laid in impenetrable taiga by resolute people who had brought cultural life to a country the size of America. Tell how wild bears in the Russian north wonderfully coexist with modern American-type steamers.

In short, we should start cultivating some kind of revolutionary and economic romanticism that would lead to heroic exploits and victories.

12. Training

Young workers and students should master the catalog of cultural setups and take advantage of it.

Mastering requires persistent exercise and *training*.

Training is needed in three areas: *daily routine, work and organization.*

121

The daily routine setup in everyday life is relatively easy. *Time logs* and *expenditure logs* will provide a framework and foster planning abilities. The *morning exercise* will charge for the day, like the morning prayer once did for believers. After these simple things are learned, the nutrition, breathing and work discipline would come automatically.

The work setup is cultivated in young workers by the factory. Students and other youth can learn it right away by organizing educational groups. Some tools and a knowledgeable man can always be found among today's workers.

The organizational setup results from the first two setups. However, it will also need the flame of real life.

The fire of ordeals and the fire of real life training grant you the right to recognition and the right to life.

The cultural set up should be put under enemy fire to inspire people and make them carefully count hours and minutes.

Our enemies are backwardness, poverty and expensive inept manufacturing.

Our cities are supposed to act as agents of culture. Yet they lose time. They can neither supply cheap goods to the village or spin it on the wheels of culture.

The moat between the city and the village is still gaping.

The village must be conquered with dexterity, organization and willpower.

Do not denounce the village.

Go there.

Take it.

Achieve.

Let us go to the village like revolutionary colonizers.

Going to the village does not at all mean we should physically go there. One can work in the city to benefit the village, though in a special way.

Go to a factory, go to the workshop. Take up the simplest job, the most primitive operation. Adjust all the tools and implements, streamline the supply of raw materials and accelerate your work. Calculate your gains, record your achievements and spread them around.

On the other hand, we should literally go to the village as well.

This policy has already been announced. We should go there with some equipment as outlined by the program. What peasants expect from us, however, is *assembly work.*

The village is largely a virgin land. Hard work in summer and winter alike is not conducive to any feverish quest for culture and technology. However, a smart man from the city instantly becomes a hit in the village.

A keen eye, a sharp mind, good skills and management talent can make wonders in the village.

The "assembly" program may include setting up a blacksmith's shop, repairs on tools, sharpening various instruments, introducing steel braces for wooden structures, developing a layout for vegetable patches and so on. Help in developing abandoned or virgin land would be am even more compelling example of culture for the peasant. Cultural methods may be illustrated by any deftly built stove, cabinet or bench, by the optimal vegetable patch layout or rational watering. If risks can be taken, use the local brook to build a dam and install a small turbine. This would be the best source of culture ever.

13. Tactics

Young workers and students should spend their summers *scouting in villages.* Afterwards, say, next summer, a tight small group should equip itself with a few valuable instruments of culture and visit the village again as colonizers.

Agents of culture should know that they operate in two time zones: making preparations in the city and doing the job in the village.

Nothing can be more exciting for a young man as this preparation for the expedition. Day after day, he would meticulously learn the daily routine, train his organizational skills albeit they are so far confined to his room, task, barracks, agency or manufacturing operation. He learns the ABC of work skills and assembly while collecting portable literature in the form of manuals.

He thus prepares for a trial by fire, for the battle with darkness and backwardness. You should know:

Work is your *power.*

Organization is your skill.

Daily order is your *will.*

This what true cultural setup is all about. And all its components taken together amount to a *cultural revolution.*

Now, after this intense self-training our agent of culture is ready to depart for the village.

Cultural agents should go through a reality check. Trained young people should be exposed to actual life. Those who have read some books on NOT should face a real linden bark shoe still worn by peasants. A young psychologist should be shown fake church miracles like, say, the self-rejuvenation of old icons. A guy who has heard a lot about wonderful machines should be abruptly put into frozen wild taiga. This attitude would mean real-life training that can be appreciated only through daring economic initiatives.

So – let's go to the village!
We will not come empty-handed. We will not bring old newspapers that peasants treasure because newsprint is so good for rolling their primitive "cigarettes".

We shall come with *luggage.* This luggage is small yet convenient. It costs more than any gold. It consists of real tools, implements, drawings, manuals and popular science books.

We may have been dazzled with rural stagnation during our scouting but now we are confident: the work area has been clearly outlined, and by this time we have learned all the stamina, skills and methods we need.

The time of trial is coming, the real baptism of fire.

From the very beginning we shall need enormous tact (no rush, no audacity), discipline, resourcefulness and, last but not least, persistence and balanced confidence.

The village will not forgive rudeness, impertinence or importunity. The village, on the other hand, will appreciate at least a nicely made wooden nail. Better come there as an unassuming expert in a modest yet indispensable trade. After that *the village will realize that it needs schools, agronomists and good roads.*

So, tightly knit and well trained *expeditions to the village* should become a grinding stone for our organizational efforts.

We need not go there as pure enlighteners, preachers or dogmatists. We must come as skilled workmen, assemblers and organizers.

Every victory, however small, must be evidenced with *artifacts and documents* rather than with an irresponsible literary essay.

The tool of your victory, the efficient implement, the plan that was adopted and carried out, some documented recognition, a book or a manuscript written in the flames of your victorious exercise – these should be *exhibited* both in the city and in the country. In the city it would convince the hesitant and the timid to become new agents, in the country it will convince the disbeliever.

Such exhibitions that illustrate the success of expeditions are the best type of *personal and collective competitions.*

Exhibitions and competitions should be open to all. They will attract inventors, organizers, autodidacts and everybody who wants to participate in this siege of the village.

14. Organization

Friends who know each other well from manufacturing, from Party, professional, cooperative, Soviet work, from studies or military service vow to unite. No large groups are needed. They better be initially small (five to ten people) but tightly knit with friendship and discipline. Such groups should focus on rigorous training and exercise.

Such a group would form a *CULTURAL SETUP STATION (CSS) with an elected master.*

The station master is in charge of general management, daily routine, training and mobilization of forces. He should also have an assistant who is nominated by the general meeting and approved by the station master.

The deputy station master is in charge of group activity records. He also provides day-to-day consultations on various issues including assembly training, tools, manuals and books.

Station members spend most of their time on *training.*

As noted above, this training covers daily routine, work and organization.

Daily routine is monitored with the help of time cards and later becomes a source of time planning, food discipline, neatness, exercising and sports.

Simple metalworking, woodworking, assembling and machine operation techniques are learned on a continuing basis and regularly tested.

Organizational skills including monitoring (photographs of the working day, surveying, planning), preparation of precise reports and drawings, "finding a way out" are acquired through special exercises organized by the group. These involve the investigation and possible improvement of shops or other departments that are conducted patiently, without denouncing anyone or interfering with work. Organizational skills also include the acquisition of *assembler's kits* financed from one's own earnings, however small.

All station members are *young assemblers.*

Training will soon reveal people's characters.

The station master helped with his deputy will gradually identify individual talents from his observations. One person could be a model *daily routine man.* Another one will mostly show constructive capacities and an aptitude for work. He will be *a man of assembly.*

A third one would excel in orientation in time and space, planning and reviewing. He, therefore, is *a man of organization.*

This will make clear the composition of the group that possibly will have to be adjusted.

In the future expedition the organizer will be responsible for orientation, reviewing and planning. It would be best for him to be the station master. The daily routine man should deal with logistics, accounting and supplies; he is the best candidate to be deputy station master. And the assembly man will do the actual work, he will be the construction worker.

Apart from practical training in daily routine, work techniques and organization, the station provides theoretical training and keenly absorbs all information available in these three areas. A *secretary* should be appointed to mobilize this information, books and appropriate experts for assistance.

This is a general outline of starting a CSS. Elections and membership will be based on the person's *record* (test results, work discipline, adherence to the daily routine and – in the future – good performance during the expedition).

Our traditions have been forged by our entire history, the history of our revolution.

Prison, hard labor and internal exile taught us how to make do with most limited means and still be relatively neat and tempered. The war and the revolution have hardened the masses of our activists still more.

In god-forsaken places of exile we faced total loneliness, Arctic frosts and incredible poverty. Nevertheless, hundreds of people acted as excellent cultural setup agents in those places.

Also, recall the fearless dirt-poor settlers who left the Russia of famines to do a wonderful job of colonizing the Volga, the Urals, Siberia and the North.

The ranks of revolutionary economic magnates are growing before our very eyes. Personally or as good team members they move forward in the name of a great cause. The future is challenging us.

Come to the ready!

To victory!

2. The Second NOT Conference and TsIT[160]

Any rigorous and impartial evaluation of the Second NOT Conference (2) requires that we first identify the stages of NOT evolution in Russia.

Only after such a historical analysis we can formulate a firm and business-like position. Any static evaluation based on 1924 trends would arguably be biased and full of major errors in history. This is why prior to reviewing and evaluating the conference we shall dwell on the evolution of NOT.

1. Pre-war period

The scientific management movement in Russia started fairly long ago. In contrast to a widespread belief, it commenced almost simultaneously with that in Europe and America in terms of theory as well as practice. We should note that scientific management in America was an natural outcome of industrial experience, while Europe thought of it as a new foreign idea and treated NOT with a measure of skepticism and conservatism, so many careless and largely unsuccessful efforts were made. No attempts to apply NOT to the actual industry were made before 1912. That year also saw first articles on Taylor's system in capitalist as well as working class periodicals (3). The capitalist authors represented the association of entrepreneurs in the metals industry, the other side belonged to the metal workers' union. (Incidentally, the famous French trade unionist Merrheim wrote the first, may we say, brilliant article about Taylor's system for the La Vie Ouvrière magazine). Until recently

---

[160] This brilliant and highly polemic paper is reprinted unabridged from the journal Organizatsiya truda [Labor Management], 1924, No. 2-3.

France made several failed attempts to introduce NOT, while scientific management experiments at Russian factories were in full swing at that time. Moreover, early scientific management applications at the Urals (Lysva and elsewhere) date back to the dawn of the XX century (1904).

The Russian engineering thought, generally speaking, is hardly conservative. For instance, theoretical motion studies were conducted by professor Sechenov well before any serious interest in this subject existed in Western Europe and America (4); a remarkable practical investigation into motions by Belavenets seems to us as good as Gilbreth's papers in terms of persistence and methodology (5).

Many prominent industrialists in Russia tried to implement NOT at their own risk. In particular, Mr. Semenov started gradually introducing scientific management at his factory that produced parts for tobacco processing machines. His attempts were resolute and meticulous in a rather non-Russian way.

Even a school of thought started emerging in Russia, as evidenced by the establishment of new university departments. For instance, professor Savin (6) carried out his lab studies with a certain mechanic at a vocational school. He published a treatise "Metals Cutting" that Western literature values now at par with Taylor's works. A special group of engineers at the Polytechnic Institute who studied Taylorism with due regard to Semenov's experience started advocating new methods of labor management. Members of this group made bold efforts to introduce NOT at other factories (such as Aivaz and Vulkan) using Semenov's experience. At the same time attempts are made to implement NOT at an artillery plant and a number of other military enterprises. Certain principles of scientific management are applied at the Urals. Finally, note a most impressive reform called "traffic consolidation" at the Southern railway. While met with certain skepticism at first, this reform soon had a major practical impact of increasing the railway capacity.

This practical movement was soon reflected in the literature. A special publishing house headed by the engineer Levenshtern (the authors included artillerists, engineers and academics) started an advocacy campaign for Taylorism and NOT in general that dwarfed any similar activity in Europe (8). Papers on Taylorism also appeared in "Russian Wealth", "The World of God", "A Journal for Everybody" and a number of

131

other periodicals. Newspapers followed suit. The "Pravda" in 1913 already wrote about Taylorism and scientific management. Even "The Exchange Chronicles" covered attempts by engineer Semenov and others.

Before the war Russia already had 8 factories where some kind of scientific management was used, in sharp contrast to the only such factory in France.

All this demonstrates that scientific management was being introduced on a noticeable scale even before the war. The NOT movement was initiated by a serious group of military and civil engineers and by prominent academics rather than by pure theoreticians.

We must add that trade unions also expressed some interest in this movement. In accordance with their general position, this interest was naturally negative. Trade unions opposed scientific management principles as a threat to workers' movement in the form of an unbearable intensification of labor. In their opinion, scientific management had to be attacked.

A strike at Aivaz factory was largely caused by the implementation of NOT. By the way, the parties showed far less animosity than in France, where NOT was introduced in a highly police-like atmosphere.

II. The war period

The factories that applied NOT before the war were mostly engaged in large-scale production. At Aivaz, for instance, it applied to just one product, the sight frame for rifles, whose manufacturing was broken down to about two hundred manual and machine-tool operations.

Other private factories that introduced NOT also filled orders from the military. No wonder that when the war broke out, both private and state-owned factories started paying more attention to scientific management as a component of large-scale production.

It was especially true in 1915-16 as the army was facing a dramatic shortage of military supplies. Elements of NOT were applied in Tula, Sestroretsk, Leningrad, the Urals and elsewhere at factories that manufactured shells, rifles, bullets, cartridges and other mass-produced supplies. It is worth noting that reform efforts focused on quality control and the development of precise gauges, templates and calibers. These processes were conducive to the creation of a school of military quality control experts who helped maintain healthy production.

Quality control with rejection of substandard items is a key indicator of productivity. Hence the introduction of quality control and guidance (continuing hands-on training) was the main slogan of reforms.

The Ministry of Defense was paying keen attention to the guidance of workmen. It turned out that many military engineers demonstrated excellent management talents. The related major efforts of the ministry are well described in General Manikovsky's book (9) "Provision of military supplies for the Russian army during the war in 1914-1918" (in two parts).

This is what Manikovsky writes about guidance in industry:

"When most of this industry was contracted by the Ministry of Defense as army suppliers, it turned out that an enormous effort and a lot of time were needed for the necessary guidance of factory engineers as well as for the education of workmen who had to get used to precision standards set for military products."
(A. Manikovsky. Provision of military supplies to the Russian army during the war of 1914-1918, part I. Moscow, 1920, p. 13).

To illustrate the high competence involved in quality control and guidance we should point out that military engineers succeeded not only in securing an appropriate supply of military products but also in training instructors who worked in Russia as well as in France and America under Russian military contracts. It was found that the management and manufacturing capacity in these countries was far from perfect? so Russia had to send abroad teams of engineers, technicians and skilled workers to provide manufacturing guidance on the spot.

Manikovsky writes about training in the American industry:

"Here are the results achieved by these prominent representatives of the much praised American industry: none of them could do the job properly. To address the situation we had to send there (under a disguise of quality control workers) our engineers and technicians specializing in relevant military industries. Only under their close control we eventually managed to set things in motion."

(A. Manikovsky. Provision of military supplies to the Russian army during the war of 1914-1918, part I. Moscow, 1920, p. 19).

Elsewhere he further emphasizes this point:

"Things, however, did not go quite as expected. It turned out that to accelerate manufacturing we had to second our "instructors", i.e. arms production specialists disguised as quality control experts, to these factories and establish a special department of arms manufacturing technology headed by Mr. Zalyubovsky, a prominent design engineer and the head of Sestroretsk Arms Factory who had just been appointed construction manager for a new arms factory near Ekaterinoslav."

(A. Manikovsky. Provision of military supplies to the Russian army during the war of 1914-1918, part I. Moscow, 1920, p. 57).

There is no bragging in this business-like book. Our own experience shows that technicians and even workmen were often sent abroad along with military design engineers.

New generation of managers came not only from the Office of military engineering but also from private factories filling military orders, including various Zemgor organizations.

In short, this movement, even if not called scientific management by many, was based on two key principles of NOT: consistent quality control and guidance that were applied on a fairly broad scale.

This work was a resounding success. While the proportion of rejected products initially could reach 80%, eventually it dropped down to a modest 5%, 2% or even zero.

Applying NOT principles to arms manufacturing was a valuable experience. We would even say that the broad trend for scientific management first emerged at arms factories, and its most talented followers came from military engineers. Our best foremen and instructors also came from those dealing with military contracts.

It was not unnatural that once the large demand for military supplies was gone with the end of the war and the unprecedented large-scale manufacturing wound down, factories started declining. While engineers, foremen and workers began losing their skills. Only a handful of these exciting people has lasted until now. We believe they may be of considerable interest to scientific management initiatives.

III.Trade union period

Trade unions also wrote a remarkable page in the history of NOT in Russia. It was not by chance that the hotbed of their revolutionary work was Leningrad. Indeed, the earliest trade unions were established by skilled metal workers from Leningrad involved in mass production of military goods. Their economic adversaries were represented either by engineers in charge of arms factories or by capitalists delivering orders for the military.

At this point signs could be seen of an orderly transition from military to civil manufacturing, with largely the same workforce as during the war. Skilled workers in Leningrad certainly took note of the enormous management efforts made by engineers in wartime. The emerging interest in management among Leningrad workmen left a certain mark on almost all the trade union movement in Russia. However, since the Russian industry outside the capital was outright primitive, Leningrad slogans were often misunderstood or misinterpreted. In other words, trade unions' interest in scientific management largely made sense in Leningrad only.

This movement started under Kerensky. In the course of collective bargaining purely economic issues such as rates and wages were automatically followed by issues of technology, work rules and quality of tools. The next stage concerned workers' welfare and work stress. Then the parties arrived at general management issues.

This trend was inevitable, and even after the trade unions' headquarters moved to Moscow, management issues were playing an ever increasing role.

During war communism labor output departments were established at industrial enterprises as surrogates for the so called work distribution departments. Their objective was to calculate industrial output norms or standard times to finish a given job. This issue is intertwined with questions like production norms, piece rates, bonus systems and others.

We would like to mention another fact that is probably not well-known.

Trade unions in their work were gradually approaching the most detailed management issues. Let us refer to a document that best illustrates the natural links between the piece rate system, production norms, the selection of workmen, administrative functions, guidance and work records.

Here is a resolution on the piece rate system passed by the Central Committee of Metal Workers on March 29, 1918.

"In order to stop the catastrophic decline in productivity and work discipline that undermines the very foundations of industry, it

is necessary to struggle for immediate changes in social policies and management systems at enterprises.

The Central Committee of the All-Russian Metal Workers Union proposes the following top priority measures: 1) adopt the piece-rate system; 2) guarantee a certain output by introducing a payment system that would closely link wages to efficiency as determined by appropriate standards; ; 3) select workers according to their skills and discipline; 4) assign administrative functions on a more detailed and specialized basis, probably increasing the number of instructors; 5) introduce the system of output records."

This resolution is a graphic example of a natural transition from remuneration to management issues. The trade union in this case acts as a producer rather than a consumer.

This resolution also illustrates how trade unions arrive at nothing else but the Taylorization of industry. In particular, they are addressing the often ignored issue of the critical input made by the army of technical personnel scattered around the factory such as service technician or foremen. At that time trade union activists obviously cared more for management issues than the factory administration did.

Administrators did not even raise such issues. Indeed, the economy was dominated by old-timers driven by political apathy rather than ignorance. No lead positions in the industry were yet occupied by vigorous new managers.

Curiously enough, trade unionists rather than administrators were the first to pay attention to the so called Taylorization and scientific management. In 1918 at a meeting with trade unionists at the Council of People's Commissars Lenin said that Taylorization needed to be introduced and tested. At that point he did support Taylor and scientific management as an industrialist. It 1923, however, as a statesman and an apparatchik he changed his mind (10).

This important period arguably ended when trade unions established the Central Institute of Labor. Little wonder that many of its active staff involved in the development of TsIT's methodology were metal workers (mostly from Aivaz) brought up in large-scale production environment.

IV. First conference

Historically, we can say that the First conference (11) continued the work of labor output departments that had taken root in the railway system (this meeting was officially hosted by the People's Commissariat for Railways, NKPS, though the initiative originally came from trade unions (see above)). On the other hand, this time coincided with an interesting attempt to organize large-scale repairs on rolling stock inspired by L.D. Trotsky. (12).

In this project Trotsky had to rely upon railway traditions and a rather small group of engineers and skilled workers familiar with the theory and practice of scientific management. One would assume, therefore, that delegates to the First conference would mostly represent railways and trade-unions. Any movement, however, has its own inertia and resonates in unexpected ways. In this case it attracted a group of biologists headed by members of the Academy of Sciences Bekhterev (13) and Yermansky who supplemented the conference with, so to say, a biological focus. An even less relevant group consisted of sociologists Strumilin (15), Bogdanov and Falkner-Smith (17).

One may say that the conference covered four areas, namely industry (represented mostly by railway workers, military engineers and several NOT practitioners), biology (represented by physiologists, psychologists and advocates of scientific management in its most general form), sociology and scientific management research (this group in fact can be regarded as the prototype of TsIT).

The most business-like resolutions were proposed by industrial workers. The most vague and romantic ones were drafted by biologists and sociologists. A few excerpts below illustrate that resolutions by industrial workers are still of practical interest.

The First conference stressed the importance of special selection of workmen. Resolution No.5 says:

"Along with the selection of executive personnel, attention should be paid to the training of workmen. Their conscious attitude to reforms should be fostered both by ideological persuasion and by improving their standards of living."

(Resolution by Section 1, Proc. Of the First All-Russian Conference on Scientific Organization of Labor and Production, January 20-27, 1921. Organization of mechanical shops, particularly railway maintenance shops. P.12).[Trudy 1-i Vserossiyskoy Initsiativnoy konferentsii po Nauchnoy Organizatsii Truda i Proizvodstva 20-27 yanvarya 1921 goda].

That very conference also passed a resolution on industrial guidance and the creation of special shop floor instructors.

«8. Enterprises using NOT should establish, in line with their specific needs:

a) training courses in shop floor guidance (including time studies) and practical NOT;

b) training courses in specific work skills;

c) model groups of workmen and foremen who have mastered scientific management practices; these groups should be used for personnel training at sister enterprises.

(From the resolution by Section 3. General and specific management. P. 122//Ibid.)

This resolution probably went unnoticed, mostly because the NKPS published the proceedings of the conference as a huge expensive volume and failed to ensure its proper distribution.

139

To illustrate the general tone set by biologists and sociologists, here an excerpt from the resolution of the plenary No.7.

"2.Scientific management must be based on the findings of psychophysiology, reflexology and hygiene regarding work processes and fatigue; only in this case it can lead to economic savings while safeguarding the interests of the working masses." (Plenary resolution. P.124//Ibid).

The vagueness of this resolution speaks for itself. Moreover, we may safely argue that any precise language in this area is still lacking today.

Now an excerpt about an executive agency.

"5. Accordingly, an agency should be set up that would rely on workers organized in trade unions to take a consistent set of measures aimed at the implementation of scientific management. " (Plenary resolution. P.124//Ibid).

TsIT at this conference mostly made presentations similar to those at the 2nd conference, discussing the issue of "how to work" from the standpoint of production activism.

Note that the 1st conference had no special section dealing with government agencies, and reports on this subject were presented at the management section.

We should note that the 1st conference produced exceedingly valuable materials that are still almost unknown not only to the scientific management public but even to many executives in charge of NOT. We believe this is the reason why so much empty talk had to be heard at the 2nd conference. If the outcome of the 1st meeting were properly taken into account, the next conference could be far more productive.

Several NOT research institutes and departments were established after the 1st conference. Most of them, however, as opposed to TsIT, belonged to the biological or the so called sociological trend demonstrated at the conference.

As a rather unexpected and unusual step, a working standards division (WSD) was also set up at Workers' and Peasants' Inspectorate (RKI). This new division has stirred the old RKI system and played a major role in attempts to apply NOT to the public service.

WSD was in fact largely modeled after the experimental TsIT station under Tsentrosoyuz that was founded in 1921.

"March 1922 saw the birth of the first NOT experimental station in Russia. It has started a movement that will certainly become a true powerful engine of reforms".
(Scientific Management. Collected papers. [Nauchnaya organizatsiya tekhniki upravleniya]. Article by N.A. Vitke. Moscow, Kooperativnoe izdatelstvo, 1923. P. 6).

WSD was obviously unaware of this event, since comrade Puchkov, one of the first TsIT activists and still the head of the station, was on leave at that time.

Now that TsIT experimental stations (like many other NOT-related projects) have become a classic, throngs of people are anxious to get some of the credit for them. Rudakov (19), for instance, claims that "I was there too!" In his version of the Tsentrosouz experimental station "it was two years ago that I proposed a slogan of organizing such stations (the first one, under Tsentrosoyuz, was founded on my initiative and according to my plan). Now this slogan has materialized in a broad network of TsIT experimental stations and other NOT units." ("Voprosy truda".

Bulletin of the People's Commissariat of Labor of the USSR. Moscow, 1924, No.3. P.72).

Rudakov's only claim to fame is his early dismissal from the station since he had little to offer except some irrelevant "plans". All the credit for setting up the station is due to comrade Puchkov.

Let us also reiterate that the first TsIT station was opened at Elektrosila factory No.5. The Tsentrosoyuz station followed. Rudakov happens to distort reality for the sake of his own small place in history.

We would like to note that WSD's papers show a degree of similarity with TsIT's ideology. For instance, they borrow the term "social engineering" from TsIT:

"A new special science is emerging, namely social engineering (applied sociology, the science of social development). It is being brought to life by the dire economic need to regard man as an active rather than passive element of the manufacturing process."
(Ibid. P. 41).

Equally illustrative are WSD's observations on the links between social engineering and education:

"Today's teacher or trainer must be a true educator whose skills are not limited to his special subject. He should know how to deal with study groups that consist of students of various ages. In other words, he must be an engineer capable of soundly designed education sociality. In this case he would certainly be using the principles of social engineering in his trade.
Don't we see in this field, therefore, that artisan teachers are being squeezed out by scientific engineering?"
(Ibid. P. 9).

It is well known that TsIT's efforts have always focused on education as the core of scientific management.

WSD, now known as the division of administration technologies division, has been the most valuable, active and creative part of the governance reforms department at RKI.

V.State governance and Lenin

A new era in the development of NOT is associated with the name of Lenin who, as noted above, raised the issue of scientific management more than once. We need not think that the problem of RKI in the context of governance reforms was a matter of casual interest to Lenin. Quite the opposite: he had spent many years persistently addressing the issue though his findings, as history has shown, were falling on deaf ears. In 1918 Lenin thought of NOT as an industrialist. From 1919 on, however, he came forward as a public servant advocating gradual yet steady application of NOT to government. He acts as an "apparatchik", a "bureaucrat", a highly serious partisan of government reform technologies. His supporters and opponents alike interpreted his words in most far-fetched ways; only now we can make some conclusions about Lenin's main concerns in this regard.

He certainly had no immediate concerns about the general structure of government. He realized that the period of construction and major reforms was over. Any further changes should rely on a very different foundation, that is, an entirely new work culture, an entirely new applied technology of work.

Many still do not understand Lenin's position. He kept viciously attacking all those who fantasized about structure, organization and government reform. He claimed that the country has no decent human material available for that:

"The most harmful thing here would be haste. The most harmful thing would be to rely on the assumption that we know at least something, or that we have any considerable number of elements necessary for the building of a really new state apparatus, one really worthy to be called socialist, Soviet, etc."

(N. Lenin. Better fewer but better. Krasnaya Nov, 1923. P17

He had no illusions about the availability of people who are capable of undertaking government reforms. He was dreaming of a rather small number of experts.

"We must follow the rule: Better fewer, but better. We must follow the rule: Better get good human material in two or even three years than work in haste without hope of getting any at all."
(N. Lenin. Better fewer but better. Krasnaya Nov, 1923. P19)

The fact that Lenin concentrated on the technology of work while largely skipping the structural and administrative issues is evidenced with his attention to reporting, or, rather, the methods rather than the system of reporting:

The Workers' and Peasants' Inspection should study, analyze and summarize the methods of accounting, the penalties for inefficiency, the methods of "detecting" fraud, and the methods of executive control."
(Bulletin of the 2nd All-Union NOT conference, March 15, 1924. NOT in the economy and in government agencies. Moscow. NK RKI. 1924. P. 33.)

The actual work process appeared far more essential to Lenin than planning. He was keenly interested in the organization of offices:

«I believe that we should develop standards of paperwork and apply them everywhere. This is the most critical thing... The

main point is the norms, i.e. how many people are needed for a particular amount of work…"

(Bulletin of the 2nd All-Union NOT conference, March 15, 1924. NOT in the economy and in government agencies. Moscow. NK RKI. 1924. P. 33.)

Lenin emphasized that our main task was to learn obedience and the culture of good work. All the rest, he claimed, was a fantasy and empty talk:

"We do not need new decrees, new agencies or new methods of struggle. We need to check people for suitability, check the actual execution." "Checking people and checking the actual execution of orders is now, again and again, the gist of all our work and policies. It is a matter of several years rather than a few months or a year."

(From Lenin's speech at the All-Russian Congress of Metal Workers, March 6, 1922).

There is a strong trend now to figure out Lenin's views on state governance not only from his letters concerning RKI but also from all of his speeches, brochures and papers dealing with with this subject.

In historic perspective it is now crystal clear that Lenin wanted to restructure RKI so that this agency would become a certain reformer of work setups and provide work culture consultations rather than engage in large-scale reforms (20). However, Lenin's words always caused a variety of reactions. This time the strongest response came from a group that had little to do with either trade unionism or industry. A trend emerged that may easily be called "NOT-babbling" that interpreted Lenin's works in the spirit of crude romanticism. They instantly believed that a new plan had been put forward. They started dreaming of a new system of government and fancied that scientific management had already become an elegant system; the task now ostensibly was to create a

Soviet NOT, a Communist NOT. Only after this philosophical, theoretical and speculative efforts could one start thinking of the actual implementation. This "plan-mongering" approach is well illustrated with the following lines:

"If during the current NEP [new economic policy] period our economy should increasingly rely on planning, NOT must become a flexible tool for pursuing this policy."

(Torbek G. "On the 2nd All-Union NOT conference" [K 2-i Vsesoyuznoy konferentsii po NOT" // "Voprosy truda". 1924. No.3).

VI.Struggle between "plan mongers" and setup agents

What became clear immediately after the 1st conference was a fundamental difference between ideas advocated by TsIT and those proclaimed under the banner of NOT elsewhere.

TsIT came up with portable slogans that had to do with "how to work", the design of operations, workmen training, activism and persistent innovation. It focused on nurturing new people rather than on unknown new technologies. Hence its "narrow base methodology" and the establishment of experimental stations since 1921. These units (that were later reorganized as orga-stations) were instrumental to strategic objectives such as fostering mass creativity, guidance, obedience and general work culture powered by will. TsIT applied this policy to government agencies as well as industry. It believed that general planning was far less of a priority than good performance and practical work methods.

TsIT was besieged by a throng of writers who pestered the institute and disrupted its peaceful work with provocative discussions and complaints to government. While TsIT was working hard on a general work setup, the plan mongers were standing up for rigid and formal planning plan as something that required a lot of theoretical cramming. School seminars, study groups, endless discussions and university NOT departments therefore proliferated. These plan mongers were addressing the most general problems of NOT, in a quest for philosophers' stone such as the Communist scientific management. They were singing mantras about streamlining, standardization and electrification that were seen as some mysterious plan that had to be fought for in a daydreaming way, almost by praying, rather than dealing with practical tasks. Incredibly, they also confused scientific management with the old-style occupational safety efforts that were aimed at protecting the workman from production rather than organize the manufacturing process. Hence their undue attention to problems of fatigue; an ominous aspiration for denouncing rather than building; all those "planning bureaus" and "study groups" - and a powerful drive for merging everything without any regard to the simple fact that whatever little had been done in terms of NOT in Russia largely remained on paper.

Hence the persistent and almost tiresome urge to regulate something.

The struggle against TsIT and its practical setup methodology started as early as 1921 within the institute. It was triggered by Shpilreyn (21), Torbek and Rudakov who kept dreaming of a sociological component added to NOT and other intricate matters. Yermansky, who by that time, it appears, was a professor teaching a NOT seminar, followed suit. Apart from criticizing TsIT, he also submitted his projects for reorganization of the institute to the authorities. He was joined by Burdyansky (22), Shatunovsky, Kaplun, Shitikov and, most recently, Radus-Zenkovich (23) and Kerzhentsev (24).

Most curiously, whenever TsIT came up with a practical move and its implementation, its critics just suggested an "opinion" on its work rather than a feasible alternative.

Here is a sample document from the program of the so called Conference of Moscow Communists actively interested in NOT (the already familiar Rudakov, Torbek, Shpilreyn and others):

"II. Scientific organization of work approaches the issues of labor and education to train workmen in the most rational, economical and healthy labor practices, using for this purpose all the findings of studies on labor processes, psychophysiology and modern experimental education. New training methods should always take into account the above-mentioned trend in modern industry, the creation of a skilled, highly intellectual and advanced worker who is capable of operating complex mechanisms and move quickly from one machine to another.

Therefore, training should focus on the basic principles of modern technology. The workman should be brought up as a conscientious member of the production process and the entire national economy. Along with the general physical training, in addition to learning particular skills one should develop higher psychophysiological and intellectual abilities and master the best work practices."

(Our platform in the scientific organization of labor. Abstracts for the conference of Moscow Communists actively interested in NOT. "Pravda," January 11, 1923. January 11. No. 6).

Whereas TsIT is teaching specific techniques and has a practical methodology, this resolution offers an *"introduction to the basic principles of modern technology,"* like the cute old Russian intelligentsia did in its quest for "enlightening the people". Say, TsIT discusses the issue of chiseling. It never occurs to our critics to base their arguments on an alternative technique such as cutting. They have a purely literary reaction. They just claim "it's no good" and make a fuss up to the highest levels of government.   Here is one of these literary exercises:

"In particular, it is necessary to pay particular attention to:

A) studies on work techniques [at TsIT] are limited to primitive muscular operations (chiseling and filing), which exaggerates their relative importance in manufacturing and diverts the attention of NOT experts from improvements in machinery and the mechanization of production;

B) psychophysiological aspects are all but ignored in labor studies; occupational safety issues are disregarded; interests of production are opposed to those of the proletariat in a non-communist way;

C) the training system handles the workman as a circus animal, subduing his interests to the idolized production process; a living person tends to be turned into a thoughtless and dumb executor without any general skills and adequate universal knowledge."

(Our platform in the scientific organization of labor. Abstracts for the conference of Moscow Communists actively interested in NOT. "Pravda," January 11, 1923. January 11. No. 6).

We see that their inspection of TsIT resulted mostly in annoying fiction exercises or just "general observations.".

Let us now turn to some historical evidence illustrating the atmosphere in which TsIT had to carry out its setup work.

I must say that the debate around TsIT at that time was much complicated by P.M. Kerzhentsev who had, as if on purpose, just returned from abroad and soon became a rather prominent expert in scientific management. Two demons fought in his soul. On the one hand, he was exceedingly fond of TsIT, its drive and persistence. On the other hand he obviously wanted TsIT to be more docile. At times it seemed to him that, in general, whatever little disagreement there is would vanish shortly. For example, he wrote:

"In general, the differences between Gastev's supporters and the Communist group in due course will be reduced to minor tiffs rather than lead to a significant and profound schism."

(Kerzhentsev P.M. NOT (Scientific Organization of Labor). M.-Pg. Gosizdat. 1923. Pp. 20).

Soon, however, he found himself inside a fatal square whose four corners were occupied by RKI, the Time League (25), TsIT and, finally, student study groups once inspired by Yermansky.

Kerzhentsev wanted to be in the middle of this square. He first tried to influence the RKI but without any luck. He tried to talk to students but found them too much into Yermansky's philosophy that he disliked. He started a "social" movement, the Time League, but instead of doing practical work he began firing at TsIT. This is what he came down to:

"TsIT's deviation bears the stamp of petty bourgeois perversion of Taylorism with the actual advocacy of backward technologies. It also treats the entire issue of scientific management from the standpoint of the individual worker.

Also, TsIT significantly breaks away from industrial practices and belittles the importance of production aspects; it brushes aside management issues, particularly those related to the reorganization of government; it associates scientific management with a number of irrelevant problems ("economic scouting", "cultural setup", etc. .); it declares the "narrow base" principle as a universal NOT; finally, it carelessly transplants methods of technology and biology to the domain of social phenomena. "

(NOT in the USSR. Reading notes for the 2nd All-Union NOT Conference. "Pravda" 1924. Feb 13. No. 35).

His animosity was growing further. He pretended to be unaware of past attacks on TsIT and opposed the piece rate system.

"5) Speaking of wages, the piece rate system that is based on bargaining with the worker on every job must be eradicated."

(NOT in the USSR. Reading notes for the 2nd All-Union NOT Conference. "Pravda" 1924. Feb 14. No. 36).

This nonsense was written in 1924.

Regarding the need to intensify production, Kerzhentsev rallied with students raised on Yermansky to oppose labor intensification. While being completely unfamiliar with the practical ways of scientific management, he began to criticize the idea of shop floor instructors that TsIT ostensible designed to become some kind of aristocracy.

"6) The question of raising productivity without labor intensification and the link between wages and productivity should be put forward as a particularly important practical problem."

(NOT in the USSR. Reading notes for the 2nd All-Union NOT Conference. "Pravda" 1924. Feb 14. No. 36).

"Thirdly, TsIT suggests that working class aristocrats, scientific management priests should be trained."

(Kerzhentsev P. Two platforms on NOT: For discussion. "Trud"". № 41, February 20, 1924).

More and more mesmerized with his own agitation, he came down to the following:

"Oh Taylor, I recognize you! TsIT has learned well your attitude to the workman – with condescension, with some money in the fist, with mysterious formulas and little confidence in his consciousness."

(Kerzhentsev P. Two platforms on NOT: For discussion. "Trud". No. 41. February 20, 1924).

These panic words were the ones that ultimately drowned Kerzhentsev...

Sometimes he got carried away with agitation and spoke with a remarkable anger:

"Yes, we shall continue fighting with comrade Goltsman (26) and others about the program particulars and the entire platform, because their theoretical blunders and deviations have dangerous practical implications for work on NOT, for the cause of economic recovery in the country, for the correctness of the proletarian position."

(Kerzhentsev P. Two platforms on NOT: For discussion. "Trud". No. 41. February 20, 1924).
The "fight" did take place without bloodshed, but cost a lot of ink and tears.

Comrade Rozmirovich gave him a reasonable and balanced answer. She noted that this attack against TsIT was also aimed at the RKI strategy (which later turned out to be the case).

"Everything in the platform of the Communist group is directed against the so-called "narrow base "as a generic NOT method used by TsIT and RKI."

In the course of their fight with this principle they have added a lot of quite meaningless phrases and provisions to their platform. "

(NOT from the standpoint of further development of the revolution: On the NOT platform of a group of Communists. "Pravda". 1924, February 21, No.42. - E. Rozmirovich).

Yet Kerzhentsev's writings were relatively innocuous. To show the environment in which TsIT had to live, let us quote the following passage from a specially published "scientific" book by Burdyansky, director of the Kazan Institute of Labor:

"In conclusion, I am confident the relevant authorities that will soon start to coordinate all labor research institutions will turn their attention to the toxic ideology(both from the technological and the political point of view) disseminated by the Central Institute of Labor, and will change the abnormal situation where an institution financed with proletarian money conducts a business in the RSFSR that would be gladly paid for by the occupiers of the Ruhr basin who pay handouts to Russian counterrevolutionaries."

(I.M.Burdyansky. On one reactionary ideology. [*Ob odnoy reaktsionnoy ideologii*] "Voprosy NOT." Reprint from the magazine "Communist Path", № 2, 1923.)

This brochure was printed right before the 2nd conference in 500 copies as another bomb against TsIT. Whether the publication was financed by the proletariat or personally by Burdyansky remains unclear.

Not only did he write the brochure. His institute obviously saw this publication as a matter of high priority. It sent a circular to senior government officials, members of the Cabinet and members of the Central Committee of the Communist Party. We are quoting this letter, signed by Burdyansky himself, verbatim:

"All-Union Central Council of Trade Unions, comrade Senyushkin (personally).

In connection with the your nomination to the Board of the Central Institute of Labor (the "Trud" newspaper No. 56, March 14) the Kazan Institute of Scientific Management feels obliged to send you an article by its director I.M. Burdyansky "On one reactionary ideology. "Voprosy NOT." Reprint from the magazine "Communist Path", № 2, 1923.
Attachment: as mentioned.

Director of the Institute, a member of the Presidium of SUIT (Burdyansky)

Secretary: (Yasinskaya).

(The Tartar SSR. People's Commissariat of Labor. Institute of Scientific Management. March 17, 1023. No. 157).

No response to the brochure or the letter followed.

A lot of time was also wasted by another leader of this group, Shatunovsky. Here is his most recent literary exercise:

"A. Gastev, his ideology and his institute are like foam on the crest of the production wave of our revolution. Foam is always on top but not everyone can realize that it is nothing else but foam. "

(Ya. Shatunovsky. Scientific organization of labor and its anarchist interpretation. [*Nauchnaya organizatsiya truda i ee anarkhistskoe vyyavlenie*]"Krasnaya Nov", No.6. 1923. P. 252).

Here is another passage that is just as fascinating.

"So, Lunacharsky (28) should be demoted. Durov the famous clown should become the People's Commissar for Education instead. Let us launch the production of circus whips to replace textbooks. Well, since man differs somewhat from animals, the circus whip may be replaced with special Cossack whips."

(Ibid. pp. 255 and 256).

And the final stage of this vicious mockery is:

"Gastev would better take a stick from his "culture setup kit" to kick all these Robinsonian fantasies out of his head."
(Ibid. p. 261).

We had no time to answer such arguments. In a nutshell, however, the following statement conveys our opinion on Shatunovsky's exercises:

"Of course, any major new project generates not only supporters and serious opponents but also clowns. No doubt that conspiratorial nihilism as a methodology must have its own choir and its own master."

(Gastev A. Conspiratorial nihilism as a methodology. [Shatunovschina, kak metodika]. "Krasnaya Nov " 1924, No.1. P. 238).

Regrettably, such criticism worked to inspire not only those comrades who called themselves NOT Communists but also certain professionals who also used to their academic knowledge to sting TsIT on occasion. For example, here is an exercise by one professor Sokolov:

"Take a shipyard building a dreadnought. Its tower alone needs a venerable 42,000 parts. With ten operations per part the total number of operations is 420,000. If research into just one operation, namely chiseling, took TsIT three years to complete because it involves 64 separate studies, a full study of manufacturing one tower would require 1,260,000 years. This is clearly a wrong attitude. The "narrow base" in this situation becomes infinitely narrow. I do not mean that this approach has no value whatsoever. For instance, TsIT has used it to develop a training methodology, a nice achievement probably worth the money. On the other hand, training has produced no tangible results at a single factory or government agency.

The broad base method features none of these drawbacks because it aims at covering the entire enterprise in terms of structural units."

(Sokolov B.G. Two trends in NOT [Dva techeniya v NOT]. : Voprosy truda." Moscow: NKT. 1924. No. 1. P. 68).

I bet that Professor Sokolov, whether he is a mathematician or a NOT scholar, has never seen all the operations he was talking about, since this – at 10 minutes to study each operation – it would require 24 years at eight hours a day without any Sundays off.

The following gem by Shitikov the Thunderer falls into the same category of criticism:

"In this regard, in relation to the overall organization and the technological excellence of our socialist economy, we repeat, in this respect, TsIT with all its laboratories is a nonentity and a waste of public funds. As for its physiological laboratories, they also have no links to industry and hence are of no major importance. Mind it, TsIT experiments do not come cheap. They cost over three and a half years of work by a hundred people, or 350 man-years."

(Shitikov (Samartsev) A. NOT, industry and technology [*NOT – proizvodstvenno - tekhnicheskiy*]. "Voprosy truda." Moscow: NKT. 1924. No. 1. P. 72).

We would really love to ask both Professor Sokolov and Shitikov, the modest metalworker, how much quality time was taken away from TsIT by its struggle against the numerous "NOT babblers."

Of course, none of them had any idea that their feast would end in disaster. Their course of action was "war until the full victory."

VII. Convocation of the 2nd Conference

The 2nd conference was prepared by "plan mongers" whose methodology rejects the very idea of setups. Despite the fact that all invitations to the conference were first signed by TsIT, our opponents were so intrusive that TsIT could not fully participate in the preparations. Moreover, the entire group of "plan mongers" was headed by the Labor and Industry section and its leader Radus-Zenkovich (none else but Torbek was his deputy), an old adversary of TsIT. TsIT could clearly response but with due restraint. The invitees were selected liberally. A childish presentation, some stuttering of a reading note or a plan would suffice to be admitted.

Experts with ample industrial experience were extremely scarce.

In fact, the conference was a meeting of Muscovites, mostly telling a lot of awesome and scary things about NOT. Everybody was looking forward to the first time the word "seventeen" would be uttered. As it turned out, the most aggressive warriors such as Kerzhentsev just kept silence, though he certainly knows a great number of "organizational principles". The Time League, that had already ended its fetal period and turned into the NOT League, was also mysteriously silent.

Burdyansky made a report on the types of government agencies and their restructuring "in general terms." Shatunovsky talked about social engineers. His main thought was that social engineers as such do not exist yet but this profession absolutely must be introduced by decree. Here is his charming syllogism:

"2.No such specialists are trained anywhere.
5. Social engineers are almost non-existent.
Proposals: 1.Establish the profession of a social engineer by decree. "
(Shatunovsky Ya. On experts in social engineering [O spetsialistakh po sotsialnoy inzhenerii.] / / Second All-Union Conference on NOT: Abstracts of presentations. Issue 2. P. 79).

This does not come from a Young Communist's scrapbook. This is an abstract of a presentation by a keynote speaker.

Compared to the 1st Conference, the 2nd meeting shows a striking absence of meaningful practical growth. Most of the youths who convened at the conference (and indeed, some of the elders) have forgotten the vast body of experience available from the military and from the railways.

Industry-related reports somehow drowned in the sea of nightmarish babble. Happily, the conference was saved from a hopeless disaster by comrade Kuybyshev (29) whose presentation marked a turn to actual work.

Yet a fatal mistake was made. Instead of delving into the priceless experience of the military and the railway industry, the invited compilers and NOT "journalists" shouted down whatever serious reports and discussions.

Our current task does not involve a meticulous review of all the outcomes of the 2nd conference. Let us focus on its general description.

VIII. Plenary decisions

Comrade Kuybyshev's theses certainly did not come unexpected. Prior to the Conference, the All-Union Congress of Auditing Commissions had already demonstrated that the head of RKI, as a highly responsible person, did not agree with the so called plan mongers. Here is a quote from his keynote speech at the Congress:

"Research into scientific management cannot be merely academic. It should combine business-like experiments and theoretical conclusions."
(Transcript of the All-Union congress of heads and representatives of auditing commissions. February 3-4, 1924. Published by RKI of the USSR. P. 13).

Elsewhere he stresses the importance of the human factor in NOT:

"This goal would be easier to achieve by workers with good skills. Such skills or techniques used by the best workers must be accurately described, studied and used as a model."
(Ibid. P. 17).

And here is a serious warning for all those who like to act in thoughtless haste without attention to details.

"Attempts to rush government reforms must be stoppe
d. Governance should be improved in a sound way to make it more appropriate for the proletarian dictatorship."
(Ibid. P. 21).

NOT babbling is done with.

The plenary resolution passed by the Conference on comrade "Kuybyshev's report affirms most definitely that no system of scientific organization of labor has been established so far in the country. Such a system in place, however, had been considered a prerequisite for a specific Soviet NOT arrangement based on literary exercise. Here is the appropriate quote:
"We must categorically reject any attempts at interpreting NOT as universal system of labor organization."

(Resolutions of the Second All-Union Conference on NOT. Theses by comrade Kuybyshev. March 16-19, 1924. M. 1924).

A blow to plan mongers

All further provisions are not written in a calm tone. They are rather temperamental, which betrays a desire to give a strong rather than reserved rebuke to all those fiction-based games that preceded the conference. The theses bluntly claim that any talks about a specific plan for the development of NOT should be dismissed.

"The first and major work in the field of NOT in the Soviet Union, as applied to the development of the productive forces of the country, was the plan of electrification (GOELRO). Its implementation will take years, maybe over a decade, and any research in this area can only deal with improving this plan. Any deliberations on the application of NOT to economic planning, state governance and so on should be resolutely swept away as completely meaningless, if they do not refer to the development and implementation of this plan."

Work with what we have. A blow to machine romanticism

Daydreamers' expectations of a machine that would arrive as a savior, would not require any skills to operate and would not use muscular labor (fi donc!) are challenged in a realistic and balanced way with the idea of taking advantage of the available equipment and continuing the specific work processes of today rather than dreaming of those to come. Many a NOT scholar regard the machine as if they were Chekhov's characters in "Three sisters" looking at "the sky in diamonds". In response to this limp and disarming perception of the machine which "will come once" as opposed to that boldly and carefully designed Kuybyshev puts strong emphasis on the following:

"If we cannot quickly pursue the path of mechanization and electrification in the country, we can and must (this is required to compete with private capital) to embark on the track of sound organization of labor within enterprises and institutions. In this area NOT has an unlimited potential. Since our technological culture is low, economic resistance to the capitalist West, competition with the private businessman and, most of all, a gradual increase in national wealth all require an increase in productivity. To this end, the scientific thought and the workers' initiative must focus on improving the efficiency of existing equipment, on scientific management at enterprises and government agencies; rational organization of labor at enterprises and public institutions. This cause will enjoy strong support from industrial actors who, under a dictatorship of their own class, are interested in the recovery of their enterprise as well as the national economy."

Focus on live labor

In strict accordance with these views, the theses powerfully turn the heads of "NOT babblers" and fiction writers to the real live labor. Here Kuybushev does not spare all those who ignore this issue in today's situation, when 10 kilometers away from Moscow peasants still wear linden bark shoes and value a nail as a miraculous icon.

"In this political and economic environment, any disregard for the efficiency of human labor in a country where it is especially critical because of underdeveloped technology should be viewed as childishness, or a misunderstanding of the tasks of the working class, or a disguised struggle with the proletarian dictatorship."

Intensification of labor

And then the theses are heading in a certain direction like the cogwheels of a working machine. In contrast to careful phrases that sometimes touch on this delicate issue and sometimes ignore it, Kuybyshev definitely states that labor intensification is a must. At this point, we should expect many more disputes on whether this intensification means squeezing sweat from the workman or it may result from special training to teach people make more motions while spending less energy. Even proper rest requires certain skills to be taught. We must learn to have more stamina rather than throw passive advice like "don't get tired", "have more rest" and so on.

"It would be a mistake to fundamentally deny that the intensity of labor may be increased in sectors where it lags behind that in capitalist countries. Labor intensification under the proletarian dictatorship is not the exploitation of the working class. Rather, it follows from the efforts of the working class to defend its economic position conquered from the bourgeoisie."

Natural link between wages and higher productivity

Many believe that scientific management should be introduced for esthetic reasons, just because it brings about an elegant organization of labor. Therefore workers should be urged to increase yet keep silence about the very real issue of remuneration. (Just recall how Kerzhentsev the esthete dropped phrases about TsIT that ostensibly comes to the workers "with money in the fist.")

The theses emphatically link wages to productivity gains. They underscore the tradition that was learned by trade unions as long as eight years ago.
"One of the most important means to increase the productivity of industrial labor is the introduction of a payment system that stimulates the worker to improve his factory."

Personal and group incentives

This view is further developed as the incentives principle.

"Broad attempts to remunerate good performance by individual employees as well as gangs in factory shops, at enterprises and institutions should become a current objective; performance in various sectors should become a subject of general interest, comparison and scrutiny; outstanding workers should be promptly rewarded."

Recognition of guidance. Guidance is linked to incentives.

The issue of guidance that used to cause so much controversy and fiction writing is now resolved once and for good.

What was said at the 1st conference by delegates from industry has been definitely approved, just like the idea that both the worker and the instructor must be remunerated for every success.

"The very restructuring of enterprises, if aimed at long-term improvements rather than limited to following some specific recommendations, may require the participation of shop floor instructors. They should be trained at special courses or promoted from local workers. They should also be appropriately paid. The emergence of such personnel along with an incentive system for the rest of factory workers will be a solid foundation for better productivity; moreover, less efficient workers, apart from monetary incentives, will have a good example to follow."

More about guidance. More about incentives. Active involvement of trade unions.

The idea of guidance is literally ubiquitous in comrade Kuybushev's keynote speech. In the following passage the instructor movement is linked to the initiative and energy shown by trade unions.

"The orderly involvement of trade unions will most likely help promote most gifted workers to higher positions such as instructors, service technicians, mechanics and so on.
While continuing to select people with management talents, particularly among workers, for promotion to administrative posts, the unions should now set an objective of selecting and creating a junior management force.

This selection should be based on management and production objectives at a given enterprise. Look for workers who know how to conveniently organize their workplace, who are capable of sound planning of their operations, who can improve their manual and machine-operating techniques, who produce few rejects and so on. The combination of guidance with monetary incentives provides trade unions with an opportunity to take systematic part in labor management. Trade unions can make a particularly valuable contribution to the fair payment system that remunerates workmen who discover better work techniques, suggest technological innovations or practical measures to improve efficiency (at the factory, at their shop or in their gang). "

Recognition of trade unions' initiative in labor management. TsIT as a brainchild of the unions.

The above-mentioned inherent connection between labor management and trade unions has been reiterated in several paragraphs of the resolution. Likewise, it was recognized that TsIT's cause is naturally connected to unionist practices.

"Participation of unions in this work is facilitated by the fact that they have already shown a lot of initiative in the area. In fact, the very idea of scientific management was launched by the union of metal workers followed by the entire All-Union Council of Trade Unions.

Unions came very close to scientific management issues in their work on payment systems. They have launched the slogan of introducing production norms and established factory labor standardization divisions as a certain form of labor management in Russia

Finally, unions also put forward and implemented the idea of scientific management research by establishing the Central Institute of Labor. "

Individual labor processes; operations; techniques; still more about guidance

As if to additionally endorse the setup policy as opposed to the "plan-mongering " approach, the resolution approves and legitimizes the practice of focusing attention on the labor process, on an individual operation, on the technique. All this is closely linked to the idea of guidance.

"d) it is especially critical to pay attention to practical experimental studies of industrial labor, management and individual work processes.

e) it is necessary to organize schools for the training of instructors capable of fostering best practices and innovative management under the existing conditions. Special attention should be paid at hands-on training of factory vocational school students in best work techniques and the basics of labor standardization."

This plenary resolution is the best guiding principle for further work.

This resolution unequivocally endorses the policy developed by TsIT with such great difficulty in an atmosphere of bullying, scheming, harassment and denunciations.

IX. Other speakers on TsIT

TsIT did not try to submit a large number of reports. If we wanted to compete with that huge list of presentations at the conference, we would, of course, say a word on every issue. But we did not endeavor to emulate that amateur mobilization that was demonstrated during conference preparations. So our contribution was limited to a few practical monographs and general methodological reports.

TsIT's presentation was made on a day towards the end of the conference. The event was much anticipated.

Of course, the outcome of the fight around TsIT was far from obvious. In any case, in any case our presentation was expected to be the most dramatic event of the entire conference. A certain kind of mobilization took place by that day. And dramatic it was indeed.

TsIT's presentation was attended by a large number of opponents who probably were invited on purpose.

TsIT had an opportunity not only to demonstrate its achievements but also introduce the audience to its general philosophy. Discussions on its papers proceeded as follows.

The enlightened Professor Sokolov was the first speaker who shared his historical estimates of the number of years that TsIT would need to complete its research. However, this time professor Sokolov was unusually modest and his main message was that of support.

"Comrades, what TsIT said in their reports would take much more time to discuss than five minutes. I just have to stress that TsIT has done a lot in the field of guidance and I think we can safely believe that many of these findings could greatly benefit factory-based vocational schools. "

In the second part, however, he chose to provide a detailed critique of the so called barographic method used by TsIT.

The next speaker, Bogdanov, was in a bellicose mood. He bluntly claimed that:
"As far as we can notice, all TsIT efforts completely lack a methodology. Indeed, we do not see any methodology in their work, comrades."

His evidence that was meant to expose the flaws in the setup method, however, was limited to small particulars. After his speech the entire audience was on alert for imminent heavy shelling.

Shatunovsky made a rather solemn speech. However, its first part came quite unexpected. In an insinuating and peaceful voice, he uttered:

"Comrades, I note with satisfaction that the statement made by Comrade Kuybyshev at the beginning of our conference to the effect that an agreement has been reached on our scientific management work, is materializing. In these terms, I am theoretically satisfied with comrade Gastev's report."

These words sounded much like probing the atmosphere. Since Shatunovsky is even better known for his psychological attacks on TsIT (i.e. appeals to the authorities) than theoretical debate, the above statement appeared opportunistic. Warmed up with the opposition's smiles, however, he resolutely moved on to criticize our famous chiseling studies. On this particular occasion his most compelling argument sounded as follows:

"One of our best managers, Comrade Nogin, chairman of the textile syndicate, recently visited America with a group of engineers and carefully examined a number of factories that he was particularly interested in. At his presentation about the trip for the textile workers' union he noted that chisels and files are banned in America." (When proofreading the transcripts Shatunovsky indicated that he referred to textile machinery. This did not make his wisdom less apparent, however.)

His words about chiseling in America made some in the audience laugh.

It must be admitted that Shatunovsky's speech in the context of other presentations left an impression of a probing exercise.

Shpilreyn said some highly reasonable words. He probably has had a certain crisis since he switching from crude general research into metalwork to studies on individual work operations. He unequivocally stated that:

"Any criticism that will be heard here must be friendly rather than destructive."

These words demonstrated there was no consensus on TsIT in the Group of 17.

Shpilreyn's criticism of TsIT was extremely cautious. For example, he asked:
"I wonder if the methodology that has just been demonstrated was based on research by all TsIT laboratories or discovered intuitively, as comrade Braginsky, a TsIT fellow, wrote in the magazine 'Issues in Soviet Economy and Management'? "

Unfortunately, we had no chance to answer this smarmy and polite question at the conference. So let me tell you now that intuition was indeed a factor in the development of our methodology. Other TsIT laboratories made no substantial contribution to this process, since they have been dealing specific industry standards rather than this particular approach. This, however, does not diminish their efforts because they were developing methodologies in specific other areas.

Verbov, who was speaking after Shpilreyn, is a new and original NOT figure. This medical doctor decided to study existing industrial work techniques and select the best ones empirically. His main point on TsIT was:

"What we have heard and seen here makes us believe that TsIT must certainly be credited with developing a most serious scientific methodology."

Later, however, he made a few specific critical comments, particularly on the myographic method that he considered obsolete:

168

"This is not *the latest* achievement to be proud of: *it seems pretty like a* vestige.*"

The last part of his speech was heavily laden with academic rhetoric, something pretty uncommon in our circles. He seemed to deny any value to the laboratory method and contrasted it with his own shop floor studies to find the smartest and the most efficient worker as a model.

"But in this case, at a time when we are struggling for scientific management, it is delplorable that over the past four years TsIT moved away from the mainstream and restricted its work to a kind of research that is generally a luxury for NOT scholars."

Apparently, comrade Verbov has never heard about TsIT's work at factories and institutions.

At the same time he apparently (without being aware of it) continues the tradition of Taylor who bet on the best existing worker rather than tried to create new and superior work techniques.

Comrade Kulitsky had the following intriguing words to say:

"All TsIT reports were highly focused and rich in concentrated thoughts. The mass audience tends to take this thought-saving approach for granted. In fact, a serious attitude must be fostered to achieve savings in intellectual and physical work. Today's presentations resulted from concentrated yet almost invisible work. In conclusion, I wish TsIT to continue its good work that demonstrates us how to make labor easier."

His statement, I think, expressed the opinion of a certain group of professionals who used to treat TsIT work with certain skepticism. Rudakov, the next speaker, surely talked again about that same chisel:

"TsIT has its own history and its own method. Its history is over three years long. Its method is training workers in chiseling."

His favorite mantra about TsIT, of course, is that the institute ignores management issues. And, of course, Rudakov prefers independent "planning" exercises to TsIT's research on technology and management.

Rudakov concluded his speech with an appeal for a truce:

"We are coming from history to the laboratory now, and after we make some research I trust that we shall shake hands with comrade Gastev even though we shall arrive from the opposite poles."

Now Shitikov speaks. (Many at the conference wondered what institution he was representing; towards the end of the conference it turned out that he and Shatunovsky received "personal" invitations). In fact, at the meeting this gentleman generally specialized in comic remarks to serious reports.

As soon as he started, the audience was ready to listen to another exercise in dark humor. His first words, as always, were about how much time he spent investigating TsIT's work.

"Comrades, I have carefully studied the history of TsIT, I listened to what has been said here, read what was written here, and I have come to a rather unfavorable conclusion. TsIT keeps claiming that its studies into a single basic operation will make it understand all other operations. Comrades, what a primitive way of thinking, what a narrow-minded approach it takes to say such things."

He also made a merciless conclusion:

"[TsIT means] ...nonsense and garbage, deception and a crude falsification of vocational training and science in general."

TsIT's opponents welcomed this statement with loud applause: the conciliatory notes expressed by certain speakers were obviously not shared by the opposition at large.

Shitikov's statement immediately created a tense atmosphere. It had an effect not only on the final word by the keynote speaker but also on the next speakers.

Rubinshteyn (30) followed Shitikov with a statement that surprised both TsIT and its opponents.

"It might seem a paradox, but there is some truth in that TsIT has no narrow base available."

This statement is highly typical. It had been repeated several times by Kerzhentsev. It shows that TsIT opponents are confused. They just do not realize how the narrow base principle applied to an operation can shed light on many other issues. So now they are beating a retreat and start struggling with the expansion of TsIT's base or, in other words, against one a key element of its methodology, namely a systematic review of a large number of issues using the approach that results from the narrow base principle.

Our venerable opposition has just recently started to realize the true scope of TsIT's practices.

Here is how Rubinshteyn expands on his observation:

"How can we explain the gap between TsIT's theories and practice? It seems to me that TsIT indeed has no narrow base. It has

casually tried to solve a practical issue of cutting and chiseling and now wants to turn the outcome of this beautiful practical project into a philosophers' stone, a universal method that could be applied to the entire world and used as a foundation for sociology, culture and so on."

It is remarkable that the universal practical applicability of TsIT's narrow base method seems so futuristic to our opponents.

"Recently I read Comrade Gastev's book on work setups where the whole concept is told in plain language. But even such a clear book is spoiled by a futuristic suggestion that monuments should be erected to monkeys, dogs and so forth. "

This was Rubinshteyn's first public attack on TsIT but he had clearly been recruited in advance as a responsible organizer. His speech betrayed confusion if not fear of the powerful TsIT method that has outgrown the narrow base on which it had been developed.

Shekhvatov, the next speaker, is a colorful and dynamic figure still in the grip of labor safety dogmas inspired by Yermansky. He often goes too far in his struggle and it is under his powerful influence that the Group of 17 has been becoming more and more leftist. As a resolute person, though, he is inevitably wary of TsIT's will-based success.

First of all, he explicitly admitted the following:

"There is a clear methodology that appears quite acceptable for application at factory-based vocational schools."

He makes sure to mention "on the other hand", however.

"On the other hand, comrade Shitikov who represents industrial managers made a reasonable remark. Indeed, the words

and actions of TsIT, a major player in the NOT movement, suggest that there is no NOT but TsIT and Gastev is its prophet. TsIT's true role should not be exaggerated. This conference should sum up the outcome of our efforts in its resolutions and TsIT management should not be upset if assigned a modest spot in scientific management research."

Rather than making a case against TsIT, this passage is merely an outbreak of an uncompromising "who beats who" approach. We certainly think of it as a certain symptom.

Shekhvatov's speech that supported some points made by Shitikov sounded like a challenge, intentional or not.

The next speaker, comrade Kaplun, stated:

"I still disagree with TsIT in a number of serious ways. Yet it today's criticism of TsIT seems too superficial."

His speech resembled that by Shpilreyn. We have to note that these two major opponents of TsIT and the most independent scholars have actually stopped their warfare against TsIT. His final words on occupational safety and other matters sounded like a regular discussion at a business meeting rather than an attack.

Kaplun's speech marked a certain turning point at the conference.

The next speaker, Kizilov, an industrial engineer and an avid supporter of TsIT, said the following:

"All those accusations that TsIT has no methodology and that its research is useless sound fairly academic to me. What I see in reality is that TsIT provides a work technique rather than a training methodology. One has just to go to a factory shop and see how people work there and what they learn from TsIT. The

173

transportation sector where I work held several conferences on factory-based vocational schools and organized training that stirred a lot of enthusiasm among our semi-literate instructors. Their attitude, I trust, should mean more to us than those superficial phrases thrown today from this podium. I think TsIT has solved the problem of factory-based vocational training. We need not talk about it anymore. "

Another insightful statement made by Kizilov sheds light on the famous debate about the machine which TsIT's opponents perceive as a matter of ideology rather than design:

"I think we shall proceed from training to machine design rather than vice versa. This is why the problem of TsIT is critical to scientific management as a whole."

The speech by Noa (31), who is generally very loyal to TsIT, was also interesting as an opinion of a seasoned industrial professional. Note that his view on the machine is similar to that expressed by Kizilov, also an engineer.

"I just have to emphasize that the previous speaker keenly noted that we are facing a problem to be addressed, namely who will be building those machines."

In conclusion he made the following definitive statement about TsIT's work:

"If you approach TsIT with some practical needs, you will find the institute very useful. I think therefore that TsIT is doing a wonderful job."

Nesmeyanov (32) delivered a rather strange speech. While discussing the same things as Rubinshteyn, though in a more appropriate way, he actually endorsed TsIT's efforts.

"Despite his sectarianism, comrade Gastev will certainly arrive at the principles of tectology and broad-based research, if only he is a live human being, of course."

Perhaps he was the only speaker at the conference who happened to promote Bogdanov's views on the theory of organization. We have never argued on this issue and probably never will because Bogdanov and Nesmeyanov prefer pure theory to a constructive approach. We dare to believe, however, that in the not too distant future TsIT will have to come with an organizational science based on a system of active organizational setups rather than general mathematical or philosophical provisions.

The final speech by comrade Kerzhentsev, was hardly a surprise. On the one hand, the speaker had been virulent enough to become the leader of attacks on TsIT. On the other hand, in the more distant past he had also made numerous compliments to the institute. So he obviously decided to use this chance to get out of the unpleasant situation that he created for himself before the conference.

"Comrades, TsIT has been and probably will be a subject of much debate. The reason is that TsIT is certainly our biggest institution working in the field of NOT. I think after today's demonstration, we can reiterate my words written about 4 months ago on the third anniversary of TsIT. That is, regardless of all the past and present mistakes, the balance is in favor of TsIT. I think and I hope that TsIT owes some of its strength to the fact that it keeps paying scant attention to debate. Generally this strength comes from its major achievements in education, the principal area of research at TsIT."

It seems a little bizarre that TsIT is claimed to be strong because "it keeps paying scant attention to debate". We can only take note of this interesting point in the future and care even less for criticism that which will undoubtedly continue, especially from those who focus on scientific management of *words.*

However, Kerzhentsev, much like Rubinshteyn before him, made a provocative remark implying that TsIT should keep to its own narrow base and in no way deal with the "celestial spheres" now believed to be temporarily occupied by its opponents.

"Therefore, if the conference passes a resolution, we need to emphasize TsIT's useful work and encourage it to continue educational research rather than deal with the celestial spheres, as our comrades said."

We can easily reassure everybody including P.M. Kerzhentsev who has spent so much effort on "NOT at large" rather than the "narrow base". Sooner or later we shall reach the sky in any case without creating any nuisance to the occupants of the celestial sphere, since we already have a "setup" of our own even there.

X. Resolution on TsIT

The resolution on TsIT was reviewed by the Presidium of the conference and the editorial commission.

The makeup of votes at the meeting was unfavorable for TsIT. This fact certainly had an impact on some aspects of the conference. Comrades Radus-Zenkovich and Kerzhentsev tried to smooth over the 4th paragraph of the resolution. TsIT, strictly speaking, did not mind, because this paragraph gave priority to careful implementation of TsIT's methodology over an abrupt raid on existing factories. In any event we certainly accepted the amendments as a symptom that will obviously continue to have an impact on TsIT's work.

The resolution of the Conference on TsIT reads as follows:

"1.The Conference approves TsIT's efforts on workforce training and education.

2. The Conference particularly welcomes TsIT's methodology based on meticulous experimental studies of work operations. Experimentation should be the basis for any serious NOT work.

3. The Conference notes with satisfaction that research into primary work operations has allowed TsIT to move on to training workers as machine operators.

4. The Conference encourages TsIT to test its methodology in factory-based vocational schools and among factory workers."

The resolution was adopted at a plenary session by a majority vote of all against one (Ginzburg, employee of the Labor and Industry section at RKI).

XI. Spontaneous support for TsIT

Many believe education to be TsIT's core business without realizing that it goes in tandem with our focus on work according to precise instructions. Our special interest in education is due to the low cultural level of this country.

However, we did not want to raise this issue at all. It is no secret that TsIT made no presentations at the education section of the conference.

Incidentally, TsIT had nothing to do with convening this section. It was organized by comrade Kan (33) who vigorously advocated an immediate introduction of NOT awareness programs and NOT courses in all schools of the USSR among RKI staff. TsIT has been skeptical about comrade Kan's work, however. His concepts of education as well as industry are so naive that we have no common ground with him whatsoever. Hence we have never had any discussions with comrade Kan.

We sensed his "leadership" in those naive queries from the labor and industry section. It was not before the actual conference that the Central Control Commission appointed A. Gastev as chairman of this section. This appointment, however, was a mere formality, since neither Gastev nor TsIT took any part in preparations for the panel. This is why we were so interested in listening to comrade Kan's, so to say, conceptual keynote speech.

Even TsIT, though, could not expect what happened to Kan at this section. He suffered a defeat no statesman had ever experienced in any Parliament.

No speaker lent him any support whatsoever. Everybody was destroying him rather than criticizing. In his final word he had to admit that he "remained alone".

How come the labor and industry section did not anticipate this disaster? How come Kan managed to have a certain influence on the higher educational institutions of the country? This is still a mystery. In any event, he had to speak in an exceptionally hostile environment as the sole supporter of a system that evoked no sympathy in any of the speakers. Here are some of their comments.

"I have heard a lot of formulas at this conference. I also have a formula that describes all the presentation, a chemical formula. It is H_2O, that is, water. Scientific management cannot be taught at high school, and Mikhaylov (34) was right when he was talking about the cultural setup that we need." (Lyzlov).

Indeed, many used the word "water" to describe Kan's speech. Curiously, delegates started mentioning TsIT and its methodology favorably in their comments to this very first presentation even though there was no special report on the institute.

Shokhin, the leader of the Young Communists' movement in education and a prominent official at the People's Commissariat for Education, made an equally uncompromising statement:

"Kan was pouring water into a sieve. I propose that we elect a commission to deal with this issue."

The very proposal to elect a commission was an outrageous insult to the speaker who was sort of simply dismissed in this speech.

This incident had ramifications of its own, however.

Let us quote a few passages from debates at the education section where TsIT's ideas were discussed without any interference on our part.

Here is the statement by engineer Vasiliev (35), who made a presentation on NOT in universities:

"In this sense, we need to promote and implement TsIT's training methodology to benefit universities."

No one would expect any references to TsIT in this particular presentation, but history was doing its job.

Now, in a presentation on infantry training comrade Girs, a senior military officer, was talking emphatically about TsIT's methodology and the need to promote "new cultural setups" in the army. In his comments to educational presentations he also said the following:

"I would argue that only the laboratory approach can link theory with practice. Gastev's ideas are often misunderstood. The value of his work is that it provides a teacher with a methodology and strengthens his skills. Our questions and approaches are often

too vaguely formulated. We need to foster precision, diligence and other moral qualities in teachers, and this is where TsIT's work can be highly valuable."

This is what comrade Shokhin noted:

"In particular, it is important to implement methods developed by the Central Institute of Labor subject to a certain critical review. After an initial period of skepticism we have come to recognize these methods, considering that they refer so far to early training only and that TsIT programs should be adjusted to be industry-specific. Since old foremen are not able to address this issue, retraining them is a priority. Next spring, labor research centers should start organizing appropriate courses and creative laboratories at several factories. However, this training should avoid the cramming attitude that may well sneak into Gastev's methodology."

In contrast to the previous statements, this one is more categorical. And we, of course, think it is inappropriate to argue about those particulars or interpretations, if I may, that comrade Shokhin contributed to the discussion of our methods.

It also turned out that comrade Shokhin fully accepts the use of TsIT's method in industrial guidance. Here is the relevant passage from his report at the section:

"The next issue is as follows. Factory-based vocational schools hardly need any high-brow NOT courses. What they need is special seminars that would foster a better attitude to learning. It would be most welcome if some experts are asked to develop an appropriate curriculum covering elementary topics such as "organize yourself", "how to work" or "NOT elements in everyday life". In this regard, we can find valuable material in the resolution passed by Leningrad trade unions on comrade Gastev's report on industrial guidance // Labor Organization, № 1."

Now let us turn to comments by comrade Mikhaylov who has organized courses for instructors in Yekaterinoslav based on TsIT methodology.

"Instructors in Yekaterinoslav have welcomed the system with full support. They also acknowledged that TsIT methodology should be introduced as a whole, with possible (and desirable) adjustments and revisions made after appropriate tests."

Currently comrade Mikhailov is already working at TsIT as a most dynamic employee.

Comrade Reinberg who works at the Central Council of Trade Unions and the Department of Vocational Training made an insightful statement.

"Schools and curricula must be cleared of all garbage. Trade unions have repeatedly pointed out that TsIT method should be introduced in factory-based vocational schools (that formally report to People's Commissariat of Education) but government agencies have not reacted. TsIT methodology resolves many pressing issues, and it should be implemented, keeping in mind, however, that factory vocational training must bring up conscious workers."

These symptomatic words indicate that we may soon arrive at an agreement with the federal education authorities on large-scale implementation of TsIT methods.

Later in the debate worthwhile comments came from Zhuravsky, a foreman with many years of experience at the Urals and in Moscow, and an ardent advocate of scientific management. His statement seems as valuable as those made by the best industrial engineers.

"Routine retraining usually is not very cost-effective. On the contrary, investment in retraining based on TsIT methods translates

181

into major savings. The thorny path taken by TsIT helps solve a multitude of problems."

In conclusion he suggested that TsIT methodology needs to be studied in a comprehensive way:

"We need to convene a conference with TsIT to study its methods."

Zaydel, one of the leading opponents of TsIT, made a few statements and a presentation. Most symptomatically, speakers at the education section either reacted with silence or challenged his position.

"Comrade Zaydel proposes the following wording for p. 10 of the resolution: 'The conference acknowledges the value of TsIT's research into basic metal working techniques (chiseling and filing) but wishes to point out that a skilled workman needs more than just mastering the elementary techniques of a trade. He also needs to consolidate such techniques by more or less long practice. He also needs to learn the fundamentals of technology. TsIT's method, therefore, can be recommended for the initial stage of vocational training. It can never replace the full training required to produce a skilled worker.' Comrade Zaydel's proposal is rejected."

Apparently, Zaydel's methodology that used to be valued by industrial workers and trainers is becoming a thing of the past.

Comrade Kurepin, a seasoned trainer in the railway sector, compared Zaydel's method to ours in the following words:

"According to Zaydel's methodology, items to be filed are supplied by other workers, so the apprentice will certainly be afraid to ruin somebody else's work. In contrast, TsIT's method proceeds from the simple to the complex. Based on analysis, it is the only method to ensure the correct synthesis."

Comrade Belousov, one of the most active workers of the Central House of Communist Education, made an equally bright comment.

"TsIT's methodology facilitates the instructor's task; in a way, it trains the trainer. An experienced instructor can take advantage of it to master a truly comprehensive approach. But TsIT's narrow base approach is another extreme."

This statement may be not very conclusive but we value it because comrade Belousov is currently working at TsIT's shops.

Whenever comrade Shokhin took the floor, he could not help but talk about TsIT. Here is one of his statements towards the end of the conference:

"Factory-based vocational schools must be treated in a comprehensive way. TsIT does not do that. However, we want to take advantage of whatever useful findings it has to offer. "

He also reported some revealing experimental results:

"In conclusion I would like to mention a few figures that demonstrate the advantages of TsIT methodology over the current practice at vocational schools. We compared the performance of students of the same age at the end of the same period of training. With TsIT students, filing of plates was accurate to within 0.005 compared to 0.1 – 0.08 in the case of other students. "

Let us recall some statements by engineer Kizilov in the light of these calculations.

"TsIT methods absolutely must be tried at schools where some instructors have completed full training at the Institute. In other schools it is desirable on a full scale and fundamentally necessary on a pilot basis.

The introduction of TsIT methodology in schools would streamline the entire training process, especially at the initial stage when the student learns the basic techniques of his trade."

Here are a few figures:

"Four years of apprenticeship is too long. The Baltic Railway vocational school has brought this time done to 3 years with the help of TsIT's system. It can be further reduced as this system develops."

Note that this speaker views education from the purely industrial viewpoint. He thinks, in particular, that:

"The system calling for technicians at two levels between the integral and the hammer is obsolete. We need just one production technician as a reliable intermediary."

Let us also recall the position of the military, both the old professionals (Girs) and the new red commanders (Akhov) who are keenly interested in TsIT and its methodology.

"In this sense TsIT's methodology (analysis, standardization and so on) appears fairly sound. This approach is what we are currently lacking." (Akhov).

Such an amazing metamorphosis experienced by this section surprised and upset many delegates. Indeed, the section was organized by Kan, who, as we already mentioned, made a presentation on "water". Ultimately, however, TsIT took over the education panel even without a presentation.

This alarmed many of the group of 17, and many comrades who hardly took any part in this section (like P.M. Kerzhentsev) showed up at its final meetings when resolutions were to be adopted.

The resolutions of the panel were independently drafted by delegates rather than by TsIT. Nevertheless, they fully support TsIT's position, which is particularly true about the general resolution. At this point a certain kind of a drama ensued.

The same Burdyansky suggested the following.

"I believe the resolution should only deal with documents discussed by this section and make judgments on issues raised at its meetings. Many provisions of this resolution, however, are based on TsIT methodology that was not discussed by the education panel. Therefore it makes no sense to endorse this methodology here."

Burdyansky apparently failed to realize how embarrassing his proposal was, since the keynote speech at the section by comrade Kan was an utter disaster.

The outcome was truly unexpected. Resolutions passed by the section were supportive of TsIT without any involvement from the institute itself. We even had no need to insist of any provisions. We encouraged the opposition to propose whatever amendments they wanted. Some small changes were adopted and some rejected.

This is what we call an impartial process.

The general resolution by the education panel, also approved by the plenary, sounds as follows:

"1.The conference believes it is appropriate to introduce NOT-oriented reforms in the current education system.
2. NOT principles in education imply that (a) the training methodology should be improved to foster a calculated response system; (b) school curricula should be based on accurate calculations and (c) the training environment should be reorganized following a careful review.

3. The conference believes that some aspects of the current education system lack a solid ground and evidence-based principles. Therefore all government institutions and all-union organizations should promote NOT as part of school curricula (especially at vocational schools).

4. NOT courses should be adapted to the particular area of study, especially at engineering schools.

5. The conference finds that a soundly organized educational system requires that (a) each educational establishment should be linked to a specific social demand; (b) apart from knowledge, schools should teach skills that are needed to apply this knowledge.

6. The conference believes that the development of new methodologies and the application of best practices are a top priority for the school system.

7. Organizational and methodological efforts are especially valuable in workforce training. Good industrial management is feasible only if such training is incorporated in the production process and students graduate as skilled self-reliant industrial workers. All stand-alone vocational schools must therefore be converted to factory-based ones.

8. The entire educational system must rely on the following principle: everybody across the industry, from a workman to a senior manager, must learn and master basic industry-specific techniques. This principle requires continuity of education from the vocational school to the engineering school.

9. It must be admitted that current workforce training lacks a consistent methodology. So it is with an even greater enthusiasm that the conference welcomes TsIT's research on the methodology of teaching the techniques of various trades and recommends to adopt TsIT methods as the basis for apprenticeship and guidance.

10. The conference believes that it is appropriate to test TsIT training methods and gradually introduce them in vocational schools, especially those at factories. NOT should be applied, first and foremost, as the precise analysis of operations to determine the standard sequence of their elements and time studies of the entire operation as well as its individual elements.

11. The conference wishes to draw special attention to the retraining of vocational school personnel, particularly instructors. Such retraining should be based on methodological work by school councils as well as on special courses in TsIT methodology.

12. As a first step to streamlining production, every effort must be made to keep schools and training shops clean and tidy. Otherwise no scientific management is possible.

13. The orderly introduction of NOT started in factory vocation schools should later spread to the factory itself. Before first students graduate from new vocational schools we should promptly start the selection and training of skilled workers as shop floor instructors who would help apprentices learn basic work techniques and master them fast. Such instructors should also be capable of planning work operations and performing them quickly and accurately. The conference urges education authorities, trade unions and economic authorities to organize such training of vocational instructors that would rely on TsIT's findings.

14. The conference encourages the authorities to carefully select students for enrollment in vocational schools and calls on school councils to develop methods of appropriate selection of students for each particular trade.

15. The conference insists that elementary work skills should be mastered at regular high schools.

16. The conference notes the lack of a sound training methodology for training in hazardous trades. Such a methodology should be developed as a matter of high priority.

17. The conference believes that books, manuals and collected papers on NOT should be written for schools of various types and NOT study groups, as well as bibliographic reference books.

18. The conference believes a special education congress should be convened to discuss workforce training methodology and NOT teaching methods."

None other than comrade Isakov, one of the Group of 17, suggested an amendment to the resolution on universities that further testifies to the spontaneity of the process:

"As a first step to the introduction of hands-on industrial training at universities it is recommended that students should be trained in basic work techniques according to TsIT methodology."

The adoption of this amendment demonstrated that TsIT methodology was at the peak of popularity and had essentially no serious open enemies. Our only foes now are the emotional types like Burdyansky, Shatunovsky of Shitikov who received "personal" invitations to the conference.

In conclusion we would like to quote the resolution on military training passed by the education panel that contains additional references to TsIT.

"Military research facilities dealing with scientific management should maintain communication with their civil counterparts, especially TsIT, to take advantage of their findings in the area of NOT and sound vocational training methodologies."

XII. Recent documents about TsIT

In connection with debate about TsIT we think it would be appropriate to quote a few documents that illustrate the attitude of leading Party and government officials to our institute. It would be instructive to compare them to the documents aimed against TsIT and signed by communist NOT experts from Moscow.

Here are these documents in alphabetical order by author.

Andreev (36), secretary of the Central Committee of the Russian Communist Party (CC RCP); he had a chance to monitor TsIT when it was operating on the premises of the All-Union Council of Trade Unions (AUCTU) as well as after it moved to its own building and expanded its practical work.

"The only institution that continued its hard work in an environment of distrust in NOT was the Central Institute of Labor under AUCTU. TsIT management was dealing with practical applications of NOT and the appropriate PR campaign with surprising energy. Our findings in scientific management so far have been modest but TsIT certainly ranks first in this area." (Izvestiya, 1924, No.60).

Zinoviev (37), member of CC RCP and the Politburo. Here is a statement from his article in "Pravda" where he welcomes the idea of guidance suggested by TsIT as the continuation of its general methodology.

"Comrade Gastev was right a thousand times when he told us about his extensive plan of mobilizing these workmen (new member of the Party) to become "grassroots" production managers such as maintenance technicians, foremen, gang bosses and shop directors. These are the people who will become a personal example of improving productivity. These are the people who will also introduce scientific management on a business-like basis.

Of course, this group of workers will sooner or later generate people who would go beyond their factory to become CEOs of industrial associations and on the like. Some of them will become government officials.

We need not, however, be too hasty. The bulk of these new party members should not break up with industry that needs them so much, because state-owned industry defines the entire future of socialism."

The idea of workmen guidance suggested by TsIT was covered in several articles published by "Pravda" (official paper of CC RCP). "Leningradskaya Pravda" and "Trud".

The guidance concept has become the backbone of special "instructors councils" now operated by TsIT in Moscow and Leningrad.

Comrade Zinoviev once again expressed his appreciation of this idea in a short foreword to Gastev's paper "Workmen Guidance".

"I cannot but highly recommend this essay by comrade Gastev. I would really encourage the leaders of our growing Party cells to have this article and all the issues raised therein to be discussed by their constituencies." (Zinoviev G. February 18, 1924).

Kuybyshev, chairman of the Central Control Commission and the People's Commissar of Workers' and Peasants' Inspectorate. Here is a fragment from his concluding speech at the 2nd NOT conference where he describes TsIT in the following terms:

"The main success of our conference and an important stage of our progress, I believe, are the achievements presented to us by the Central Institute of Labor, a universally recognized research center whose contribution to our work cannot be denied by anyone. I think that TsIT will leave this conference with even more creative power and an even greater capacity for research in scientific management. The papers presented here by TsIT are the most valuable part of our overall findings in the area of NOT."

We take this statement by comrade Kuybyshev as evidence that TsIT has been recognized de jure as well as de facto.

Tomsky (38), chairman of AUCTU, member of CC RCP and the Politburo. Because of the struggle that preceded the conference we are citing the full transcript of his speech.

(Transcript of speech at the joint meeting of Central Committees of trade unions and the Presidium of AUCTU attended by NOT scholars and members of student NOT study groups – March 7, 1924).

"I am proud of TsIT, our brainchild, and I hope the Presidium of AUCTU shares this feeling. All the credit for it should go to A.K. Gastev. How did TsIT emerge? I remember Gastev's visit when he told me it would be appropriate to start studying work processes as a prerequisite to NOT research. Please take note of the word "prerequisite". We had a lot of arguments with Gastev and comrade Goltsman but I will talk about it later. I was critical. I know Gastev is a man of wide-ranging enterprise and a man of action. I told him: please start the project with small things. Here is a desk, a chair, an inkwell and a pen. Gastev spent several months with these implements. Do you think he did not try everything you are proposing now? The nascent TsIT was desperate for help. It approached Bekhterev and other professors who offered no material help. As for my own personal role, I must honestly admit that I kept thwarting Gastev's efforts by telling him: do not get carried away, do something real – and as he demonstrated real achievements, we increased our support. Many years have passed; TsIT is alive and well yet some comrades like Shpilreyn firmly believe that TsIT is far too popular and therefore harmful. TsIT is indeed so popular that some American engineers know more about it than the Russian NOT community. Gastev and TsIT should certainly be credited with organizing extensive no-nonsense studies of work motions. They should be commended even more for not losing their way and plunging into various impracticable schemes.

At some point TsIT merged with a much smaller and weaker entity, i.e. the Institute of Labor under the People's Commissariat of Labor, that dealt exclusively with occupational safety. As TsIT was coming of age in its realistic applied research and proceeding from the specific to the general, as it was studying one element to infer general principles inherent to all work motions, we assumed the role of judges and determined what was right and wrong in this process. It was after this scrutiny that comrade Shatunovsky and comrade

Kaplun complained to me that TsIT operated on a narrow scale, paid no attention to occupational safety, and ignored the fundamental issues of NOT in favor of investigating work motions. They also claimed Gastev was ruling TsIT as a dictator and did not listen to them Communists. Comrade Kerzhentsev and his supporters were professing industrial reforms "in general", contrary to the very spirit of the current economic era. It is fairly easy to write any book "in general terms" and any professional could just take a seat at a desk and promptly suggest a restructuring scheme for any government agency as an array of red and blue squares. We are accustomed to it now. Talking about "general" issues is a breeze. What we do not know, unfortunately, is how to do actual work. When told to organize work "in general", Gastev responded that investigations into practical work help grasp the whole picture. When certain comrades flashed their Party cards and accused TsIT of lacking the Party leadership, we told them that TsiT did its job, while their only advantage were these Party cards rather than a business-like program. They wanted our child to have seven nannies none of whom cared [as in a Russian proverb]. Ultimately our child was left with just one nanny. they finally dropped the occupational safety issue but started making fun of TsIT (I have heard the echo of this attitude here today) by opposing their primitive "chisel" to your "lathe and machine-cutting tool". No insult, comrades, but all this is just babbling.

I have been to Baku recently, a true mixture of different economic epochs. Here is a Persian guy transporting oil in a flat-bottomed fishing boat. Right next to him a machine pumps out oil with a compressor. Do you think we don't realize a compressor is better than a fishing boat? But to extract oil with a compressor one needs money and machinery. We drill in Baku and so do Americans, using a different technology, and again we are smart enough to understand they are doing a better job. Do not preach to the converted. We are often advised to do business the American way here in Russia, a country with four people per square kilometer. You need money for that. You remember Lenin said a few years ago that "our elementary task is to teach workers and peasants some elementary petty bourgeois values: be polite, be decent in public, do not make mischief." And yet you claim that "your studies are too narrow, which is backward and bourgeois". When you promote work "in general", when you talk about the price gap between agricultural and industrial goods, the dictatorship of the proletariat, the seven economic periods in agriculture, the need for governance reforms and so on, trying to impose these issues on our Institute of Labor, we respond: comrades, you are dragging us back. We are perfectly aware of all these theories. I could donate several plans of Russian economic restructuring with red and blue squares to a museum. Haven't you all drawn such diagrams? Comrade Shpilreyn certainly did. Suggesting to reorganize the country in a certain way is not complicated. Yes, we know that sound reforms are needed that make economic sense. Just tell us how we should proceed with these reforms. TsIT, on the other hand, does not suggest anything to anyone and it does not want to. Some people think that TsIT wants to impose its truths on society as something singular and sacred. Nobody wants that, and nobody knows the only truth at this point. The more we seek the truth, the closer we are coming to it. You, however, have nothing to show for your words.. You just keep telling that we have a bad brainchild. Fine. We did gave birth to it and we have brought it up. And you comrades are still pregnant with future ideas. (applause). Your arguments are a thing of the past. In 1918 both Gastev and Goltsman were at one pole, professing purely Taylorian ideas and advocating the piece-rate system. Ryazanov and myself, being at the opposite pole, bluntly rejected the piece rate. Ultimately, however, we had to admit that nothing would come out without this system. You all remember the well-known theses about work discipline written by me with some editorial assistance from comrade Gastev. Posted at all factories, they were urging workers to behave, not to sleep under their machines and play cards. Many theses and brochures were printed since, but nothing improved before we introduced output rates. Contrary to comrade Shatunovsky's expectations, the theses were posted on the walls but workers continued dozing off under their machines. The era of

industrial propaganda is now gone. So please do not try to today, when you are trying to enthrall us with references to books – we read them before. We heard all the slogans urging people to take jobs at railways, fly airplanes, ride horses and build steam engines. After that we did not know what to do with all those surplus steam engines. We are past this stage, comrades. Do not drag us back, we have chosen a different course. Guidance in industry, some say, fosters aristocracy. No way. If this were true, we should let the illiterate address the illiteracy problem themselves rather than employ teachers (applause). So, when TsIT offers to train a hundred workmen, followed by a few more hundred, to instruct fellow men,– what's wrong with that? We are not against theoretical study groups. Spend as much time talking as you wish. Just don't tell us that TsIT fails to implement its methodology. Don's say that TsIT does not cover the entire area of scientific management. It may be true, but TsIT still happens to be the largest component of NOT in Russia. Now, about your research into wage systems. You are looking for formulas. Fine, but until you find your superb formula leave us with our primitive piece-rate. Look for true NOT but once you find it do not claim that you did it on your own.

Comrade Kerzhentsev also said that we should go to factories and advocate work process improvements among workers. Excellent, I can't but agree. Yet before telling the worker about best practices one should study such practices. they should be studied. No one in Russia did that before TsIT, and Taylor is of course not very relevant in this country. If you think that a trade union or TsIT can convince a Russian workman to operate according to Taylor, you are wrong. The guy has to learn how to use a simple hammer before studying Taylor. When some comrade here said that TsIT and Yermansky rely on one and the same base, I suspected you apply this philosophy to your NOT research as well. No, two people may share a bench but their heads may be turned in different directions. Such definitions of different platforms are confusing. You would object that tractors and the ancient multi-course system equally belong to agriculture. I would ask you what should we study: the tractor or the work of its operator? The tractor is well-known, but if you send it to the country and it loses a single bolt, it will stop working. No doubt the tractor is superior to the wooden plow, but if some magician would give us 100,000 tractors to be sent to villages, let me assure you that 99 thousand of them would be broken to pieces, much like those that had once been imported. Your support for better tools, i.e. machines, is far less relevant than our approach to labor research.. The capitalist researcher broke down work operations into elements, and our chiseling studies demonstrated he was right. We do not mind automatic hammers – but only provided they would be cheaper to buy and operate.

No one claims that TsIT should be the centerpiece of NOT research. Lenin once correctly remarked that the more efforts in this area are made, the better. We do not at all aspire to turn TsIT into the pillar of the Universe. But we need a program of action rather than general discussions on scientific management. Comrade Kerzhentsev's theses describe something that will not materialize before, say, 1945 rather than in 1924 or 1925. But you say nothing about what we are supposed to do now. You propose no platform or a set of objectives that would be meaningful in this particular situation. Please give us a business-like practical approach instead of theories. Our trade unions treat scientific management in a pragmatic way. They are not interested in counterproductive criticism, especially when you refer to the fact that comrade Gastev, our veteran revolutionary and a veteran Party member, had once quit the Party for some reason. This in is no excuse for card-carrying communists to systematically chastise Gastev. If you produce your Party card in response to business-like work of a non-Party member, it testifies to nothing but your Party affiliation. Enjoy it but do not claim you are an expert in scientific management if you have no talent for it. While you, comrades, are giving eloquent speeches, comrade Gastev does a great job in NOT and trade unions appreciate his work. Let us stop discussing whether a platform is Bolshevist or Menshevist, since such arguments will never result in a practical program. Suggesting that our trade unions should introduce physiology-based output rates is outright ridiculous, because such rates would use the worst workman as a yardstick. They are also nothing new. They were not discovered by your Bekhterev or anyone from your group. They are just a surviving remnant of the conservative stage that we passed long ago, an attempt to drag back rather than push forward. During our discussions comrade Shatunovsky said that we would arrive at an agreement in the course of work. Hence I suggest that we approve the work of TsIT as a whole and approve the techniques that have been experimentally tested and applied. Comrade Kerzhentsev wrote a superb book but even 30 such books cannot propel our cause because they contain nothing but ideas. A NOT study group set up at the People's Commissariat for Railways seems to be good for nothing. I overheard a conversation between two commissars today who wanted this group to be closed down. Our books are good but our study groups are bad. Such mistakes are inevitable whether we work or study. But please remember that we are practitioners as opposed to you, comrades, who carry great ideas. During the war Communism period we also had good ideas on labor research to find the most efficient techniques, but only some of them materialized as TsIT.

Do seek, comrades. We won't stand in your way. We can even help you. But while you are still seeking, please do not tell us you have already found something." (applause)

Shmidt (39), the People's Commissar of Labor of the USSR, like comrade Andreev, has been closely monitoring TsIT's efforts. He has also joined a new practical initiative by TsIT, i.e. the *Society for Workmen and Managers Training and Factory Work Reforms*. Here is his statement:

"By focusing on practical NOT studies, TsIT is following a perfect course, since if NOT is limited to theoretical or

organizational issues it would yield nice yet unrealistic projects."
(Izvestiya, 1924. No. 60).

XIII. NOT research institutes

As I have said already, all these institutes (except the
Leningrad Central Labor Laboratory at Bekhterev's Institute of the
Brain) have emerged and developed after the 1st conference.

TsIT maintained little methodological or organizational
contact with these centers. In fact, we have never regretted this.
Lenin was right, we think, when he urged to "separate before
uniting." There is no need in early centralization for the sake of a
bureaucratic slogan of "unity". Various research groups should first
demonstrate what they are capable of rather than just proclaim
formal adherence to a certain methodology and ideology.

The conference gave us a chance to see these institutes
better than ever. We should note right away that all of them have
somewhat changed their position.

The Kazan institute is the only one still following its original
course. This course, however, is that of utmost universalism
without a focus on any particular area. Its research into
psychotechnics and governance remains far too general.

Indeed, the Kazan institute has produced no specific
methodology in psychotechnics or practical advice on governance.

Many of its presentations at the conference could have been
made back in 1922. They are merely generic papers on governance
patterns and standards.

As for its practical work, the Kazan institute takes its cue
from other research groups who have already started using the

methodology developed outside of Kazan. Nevertheless, the Kazan center should be commended for its energy and enthusiasm.

The Kharkov Institute, that originally had a strong inclination for psychotechnics, has recently moved on to research in governance, obviously under the influence of the Central Control Commission and RKI. Its chairman comrade Dunaevsky has demonstrated qualities that are equally valuable for psychotechnics or governance studies. His best tool is analysis. And we do care about the area where he applies his talent.

In any event the Kharkov institute has definitely changed. Now it presents itself as a kind of governance reform laboratory, which is quite symptomatic.

Bekhterev's Leningrad institute came up with nothing special at the 2nd conference. This applies to Academician Bekhterev's speech at the plenary and to the reports presented at the psychophysiological section. The resolution proposed by Bekhterev was not even brought up for discussion. It is obvious that long years of research into the so called reflexology have produced no practical results so far.

Applied research led by comrade Shpilreyn at the People's Commissariat for Labor has been narrowing down its scope from metal-working in general to individual operations and motion studies.

To be fair, Shpilreyn shows remarkable persistence in his psychotechnical studies. He keeps trying, seeking and winning. His representative at the conference made a meaningful presentation on individual work operations.

The Taganrog NOT Institute used to focus on general management problems and even linked them to Bogdanov's tectology. It seems that now it is gradually moving on to issues of reporting in industry and has even signed management contracts with a few enterprises to test its strength. Right now, strictly speaking, it is an institute that deals with economic maneuvering, an unconventional facility that can either die of win in the future (41). It operates in a perilous area but in any case its findings are sometimes quite exciting as an incredible mix of scandalous surprises and great courage.

We are closely monitoring its work in this unusual field where, unfortunately, the Taganrog institute makes little use of its well-known methodology.

XIV. Conclusion

The 2nd NOT conference benefited mostly from the same two groups of delegates as the first one, i.e. seasoned industrial experts from the railway system and military engineers. Both groups were pursuing a planned course of action and presented valuable papers.

Unfortunately, most participants were in no mood to appreciate the tradition upheld by these two groups.

The biological faction focused on education rather than the so called psychophysiology of labor. This indicates a transition from mere theory to biological activism.

The sociological faction, so conspicuous at the 1st conference, was virtually absent, which also seems to show a certain trend.

Its place was taken by new "sociologists", the new dreamers of a Soviet and Communist NOT. Their influence, however, was more pronounced in publications before the conference rather than at the meeting itself.

The pragmatic approach favored by the conference has essentially destroyed this group so it had a zero effect on the meeting.

As for the new groups present, we should single out a rather large faction of governance scholars. This new trend, however, seems to lack any methodological leadership and presented reports that mostly contained ideological appeals than solid findings. A sound methodology for such studies has yet to be found and elaborated.

The conference was also attended by experts directly involved in industry, either at pilot stations or at factories. This powerful movement appears to have a dangerous flaw, however, since presentations by some "red directors" sounded like amateur study group essays rather than business-like management papers.

The military were also quite vocal. No doubt this movement is growing, though at this point it focuses on a general quest for ideas and real progress has yet to be made.

The so called psychotechnical school did not come up with anything of interest. It looks like this field has lost some of its vigor because of an internal crisis that would probably change it completely; maybe eventually it will not even be called psychotechnics any more.

TsIT's presentation at the conference, formally speaking, was based on a certain concept. No one said that TsIT had changed its position since the 1st conference – and we think this is our advantage.

The conference has demonstrated, in particular, that the number of NOT research entities and units was excessive. While real good practitioners or methodologists are scarce, coordinators, wild denouncers and pointless propagandists abound.

While the number of NOT research centers has not grown, there is now a glut of various councils, study groups, cells and If these indicate a growing interest in scientific management the general public, it must be a good sign. There is, however serious danger that such units would produce nothing but empty discussions and hysterical accusations.

The conference has shown that people with a background in technology who can confidently work on scientific management are in a very short supply, and that we have to rely heavily on the young generation from industry. The few so called old specialists, however valuable, suffer from poor health and ideological fatigue. They are being gradually replaced with the young forces eager to tackle this new revolutionary challenge with fresh ardor. Their number is still small but it keeps growing.

Guidance in industry and management is emerging as our slogan. Only those can win who create a new motive force instead of pompous plans and foster willpower that concentrates on real goals rather than exercises in eloquence.

It is even more important to develop practical methodologies that would work in the unique and complex Russian environment.

As for TsIT, we must admit our start has been slow, maybe at odds with our character. There is nothing wrong with this, however. A careful start helped us prevent a formal or ideological takeover by superficial partisans. Our struggle has given us strength and resilience. We continue our efforts without any changes in our methodology.

It is now that our heyday is coming. (We feel that our ideas are supported both at TsIT and elsewhere). A new force is emerging under our influence.

We are now more than lab researchers or methodologists. We have spread our tentacles to a hundred of factories and government agencies. TsIT-trained instructors and management consultants are working all over the country, not only in Moscow and Leningrad. Apart from carrying out managerial functions, they are leavening production at shops and entire enterprises.

The instructors' councils that we are setting up also attract foremen and the best workmen, therefore consolidating and deepening the concept of shop floor guidance.

Finally, we are establishing an impressive group on new methodologists who have or will have completed our manufacturing and administration courses.

We have a concern, however. Despite the "absolute recognition of TsIT" mentioned by comrade Kuybyshev, we are afraid the government could discontinue its financial so that our management potential would not fully materialize.

Yet we are not losing heart.

We shall continue our struggle for the precise and broad implementation of our methodology.

We have already entered the stage when factories and agencies can clearly see that our recommendations lead to definite savings in terms of time and public funds.

We only have to organize our work in such a way (and we have already started this process) that TsIT could be financed with a certain fraction of these savings for the national economy.

PART III. Comments and information.

(1) Gastev's claim that "our red director" is a person of "enormous personal initiative" sounds doubtful at best and must be wishful thinking.

As is well-known, the Bolshevik regime dispersed most professional managers. Thousands of plants, factories and groups of companies were headed by people who barely knew the "four rules of arithmetic" but carried a party card as their only "advantage". The results of such management naturally left much to be desired. It is also clear that Lenin's point about "a kitchen maid governing the state" was a complete failure.

However, the professional incompetence of the so called "red directors" was just a part of the problem. A socialist factory manager with a brilliant general or even professional education and ample work experience would certainly have an edge over an ignorant colleague. Yet even such a manager could not be expected to produce as much output, other factors being equal, as his capitalist counterpart.

What are the skills of a good manager? First of all, he should take care of fixed assets, save materials, look out for the best combinations of labor and capital, sources of raw materials, appropriate markets and so on and so forth. In the absence of these prerequisites any production facility is doomed to inefficiency even with the most apt and diligent workforce. Capitalist entrepreneurs operating in the free market play precisely this responsible role. They are the first to bear the risks faced by the company and to gain from its success. This stressful function calls for a strong will and an ability to work as much as needed by the business.

In contrast, socialist "red directors" have a public servant mentality. Because of socialist egalitarian principles they are not paid much more than ordinary workmen, so an appropriate incentive to good management is missing. They do not bear business risks, lose little from failures and gain little from success. They are just expected to formally follow orders, which is a far cry from the art of management. Of course, some talented "red directors" with "enormous personal initiative" did exist but they accounted for a negligible minority.

(2) The Second NOT conference started on March 10, 1924 in Moscow. It was chaired by V.V. Kuybyshev. The largest of its seven sections focused on management, which reflected a growing interest in this area. The conference dealt with methods to improve governance, office work, reporting, office equipment and other practical problems. It had a telling motto: "In connection with life, for life, not separating from life!"

The conference approved a common platform and the following principal objectives for NOT:
1) adapt Western achievements in theory and practice, share best practices with the West;
2) conduct industry-oriented research;
3) establish a communications network among NOT research centers and ensure their specialization;
4) conduct experimental research into industrial labor and individual work processes;
5) establish schools to train instructors for promoting best work practices;
6) implement NOT in industry and include its principles in curricula for all types of schools at all levels of study.

On the whole the 1st conference made a major contribution to further development of scientific management in Russia.

(3) Frederick Winslow Taylor (1856 – 1915) was an eminent American scholar and the founder of scientific management. The

205

system of management developed by Taylor was widely used in the USA and consequently across other industrialized countries.

The core of Taylor's system is that an enterprise *must be organized in a scientific way.* Routine production methods must give way to a certain balanced and sound plan. Implements should be rationally designed and placed. Work motions and techniques must also be as rational as possible and therefore have to be scrutinized, time-studied and analyzed in order to remove all unnecessary elements. A workman should be issued a special instruction card that precisely sets the speed of work, its amount and quality. Special planning departments first proposed by Taylor as the headquarters of a business determine output standards, in other words, the famous *"task"* that he referred to as one of the pillars of his system. A man who fails to perform his task loses his bonus, a second failure leads to his discharge.

This *bonus* is the *second pillar* of Taylor's system that incorporated a differential rate and bonus scheme.

The next principle is the careful selection of men for a particular job.

Finally, one of the cornerstones of Taylorism is the idea of functional management that involves a number of special foremen (teachers) responsible for certain production functions.

Taylor's system, therefore, was geared to streamlining all the factors of production in order to achieve the best results with the least expense of energy and materials.

(4) Sechenov, Ivan Mikhaylovich (1829 – 1905) – an outstanding Russian scholar, the founder of the Russian school of physiology and the objective trend in psychology. Gastev's point is that his monograph "Reflexes of the Brain" was indeed first published in 1863, i.e. long before any publications on this subject in Western Europe and the USA.

(5) Gilbreth, Frank Bunker (1868 – 1924) – a leading American scientific management scholar. After learning the principles of management formulated by Taylor he continued their development through motion studies. In particular, his research into the art of bricklaying made it possible to reduce the number of motions from 18 to 5 for a much higher efficiency. His motion studies involved a photo camera and later a movie camera to draft simultaneous motions (simo) charts, a major step forward in scientific management.

His principal works (partly co-authored with his wife Lilian Gilbreth, also a prominent NOT scholar) include Motion Study, NY, 1911; Primer of Scientific Management, NY, 1912; Fatigue Study, NY, 1916, and others.

(6) Gastev treated Professor N.N. Savin with great respect and, busy as he was, found time to attend his course on metals cutting at the Petersburg Polytechnic Institute. After the October Revolution Savin emigrated to Czechoslovakia where he became the general manager and chief engineer of Škoda.[161]

(7) Gastev worked at the Aivaz machine-building factory in 1913 during his illegal stay in St. Petersburg. The factory employed state-of-the-art European technology and management principles. Aivaz was among the limited number of Russian enterprises where Taylor's system was first introduced.

(8) In 1912 Levenshtern published "The Principles of Scientific Management" by Taylor.

---

[161] Cheparukhin V.V. Émigré Memoirs by N.N. Savin [Emigrantskie vospominaniya N.N. Savina] //Russia Abroad [Zarubezhnaya Rossiya]. 1917-1939. Volume 2. St. Petersburg, 2003. P.231.

(9) Manikovsky, Aleksey Alekseevich (1865 – 1920) – a Russian General of the Artillery. In 1927 he was the acting Minister of War in the Provisional government. After the 1917 revolution he joined the Red Army and held high-level positions (Director of Artillery Department and Logistics Director of the Red Army). Gastev's opinion and evidence from colleagues indicate that Manikovsky was indeed a talented manager.

Manikovsky died in a railway crash on a business trip to Tashkent in January 1920.

(10) Gastev refers to Lenin's famous articles dating back from 1923: "How We Should Reorganize the Workers' and Peasants' Inspection" (Recommendation to the Twelfth Party Congress) and "Better Fewer but Better", where the Bolshevik leader, in full accordance with his love for "centralization", proposed to reorganize the existing Workers' and Peasants' Inspection and merged with the Central Control Committee of the Communist Party to form a super authority which would, in particular, supervise all NOT studies in the country. Indeed, in April 1923 the XII Congress of the Russian Communist Party established such a united agency with a function of leading all scientific management activities in Russia. V.V. Kuybyshev was appointed head of the new People's Commissariat.

(11) Since the First All-Russian Initiating NOT Conference played a special role in the early history of scientific management in Russia, let us discuss it in greater detail. The conference was convened by the Railway Commissariat on the initiative of L.D. Trotsky on January 20, 1921. Its formal organizer notwithstanding, the conference discussed many issues beyond those of railway transportation, as evidenced by papers from A.A. Bogdanov, V.M. Bekhterev, A.K. Gastev, M.I. Vasiliev, O.A. Yermansky, M.N. Falkner-Smith, S.G. Strumilin and others. These presentations focused of such "non-transport" areas as industrial labor management, economic planning, labor psychology and physiology and, of course, Taylorism.

The conference was attended by 313 delegates and about 100 guests who worked in 5 sections:

1) labor management in mechanical shops, particularly in railway repair and maintenance;

2) railway management;

3) the structure of management and its components;

4) labor reflexology;

5) linkage between industrial practices and scientific management research.

The proceedings of the conference were published in six large volumes that are still awaiting scholarly studies.

These materials testify to substantial disagreement among the delegates with regard to the theoretical interpretation of NOT, *particularly concerning the attitude to Western concepts such as Taylorism and the development of Russia's own consistent approach to scientific management.*

In the course of discussion on the first issue two opposite camps emerged, namely Taylorists and Anti-Taylorists. The first group (I. Kannegisser, V. Nesmeyanov, N. Gredeskul and others) tended to equate Taylorism with scientific management at large, claiming that Taylor's concepts are fundamentally irrefutable as well as universal, since they cover *all* NOT problems and may be essentially accepted in their entirety under any social and economic system.

The second group (A. Bogdanov, O. Yermansky, V. Bekhterev, P. Yermansky and others) vehemently rejected the idea that Taylorism was politically and ideologically neutral. They argued that Taylor's system cannot be equated with scientific organization of labor because it aimed at intensification of labor beyond human capacities, which ostensibly ran contrary to the values of the new Russian regime.

Note that many delegates did realize that the very idea of scientific management was complex and multidimensional by identifying "not only its economic and technological side *(like Taylor – author's note)* but also the socioeconomic and psychophysiological aspects."[162] This position was conducive to a *complex* approach to management. It was not by chance that the conference was attended by a broad range of professionals including technicians, engineers, economists, psychologists, physiologists and doctors.

The conference also raised critical issues such as the development of NOT courses and their inclusion into the curricula of various schools, as well as the establishment of special agencies to implement the results of NOT research.

As the first ever broad scholarly forum in Russia and the world, the conference was a landmark event in the early history of Russian scientific management. It was after this meeting that large-scale NOT research started in the country.

(12) Trotsky (Bronstein), Lev Davidovich (1879 – 1940) – a famous politician and statesman, author of the so-called "permanent revolution theory", one of the leaders of the October 1917 uprising, an excellent organizer, speaker and writer of political essays. He was People's Commissar of foreign affairs (1917-1918), People's Commissar of war, member of Politburo (1919-1926), one of the main creator s of the Red Army and its commander-in-chief during the civil war.

Trotsky was ultimately defeated in his struggle with Stalin and assassinated in Mexico by Mercader, an agent of NKVD.

---

[162] Proceedings of the First All-Russian Initiating NOT Conference. [*Trudy Pervoy Vserossiyskoy initsiativnoy konferentsii po nauchnoy organizatsii truda i proizvodstva*]. January 20-27, 1921. Volume 1. Moscow, 1921. P. 4-5.

(13) Bekhterev, Vladimir Mikhaylovich (1857 – 1927). Scientific management papers hardly ever mention the name of this prominent Russian scientist, which seems fairly bizarre.

Indeed, none other than Bekhterev set up the first Russian Labor Studies Laboratory in Petrograd, led the First Russian NOT conference and presented his original views on scientific management in a report "Rational use of human energy in labor."[163]

Bekhterev's concept centers on man as a sophisticated biological and social being. He believed that the principal flaw of Taylor's system was that while concentrating on the most productive use of machines, equipment and tools, it was irrational and wasteful with regard to human labor. He wrote: "This system organizes the very mechanism of work and extracts as much energy as possible from human hands by means of its differential rate schemes, yet pays scant attention to protecting the human machine itself from wear. It introduces no scientific methods to determine the threshold above which protracted work would ruin the human machine and its health." Although Taylor claimed that his system caused no excessive fatigue in workmen, "he does not even try to prove his point in a *scientific* way, and that is the heart of the matter." Therefore, Bekhterev concluded, in the long run Taylor's system had no future.

Unlike Taylor, Bekhterev always regarded the workman as a living organism, a human being with all its physical and spiritual qualities, interests and needs. Man can certainly be compared to a machine, he wrote, but this analogy should not be exaggerated since differences are way more significant in this case than any similarities. Certain scholars argued that the machine had to be operated, while man presumably "operates himself and controls his actions." [164] This is merely an illusion, Bekhterev wrote. In fact man

---

[163] Proceedings of the First All-Russian Initiating NOT Conference … Vol. 1. Moscow, 1921. P. 23-34.
[164] Ibid. P. 23.

never enjoys complete freedom of action since he "succumbs to the influence of his innate nature [...], of past experience acquired by education [...] and, finally[...], his current environment, "the given moment." The existence of such factors in human life probably supports the man-machine analogy rather than separates humans from machines.

Nevertheless, fundamental difficulties do exist between man and machine. In particular, Bekhterev noted, a regular machine can work for any period of time without any signs of fatigue, while "the human machine" (depending how long and hard the work is) after some time would feel "exhaustion caused by the wear of working tissue and the accumulation of toxic metabolic products in its muscles, i.e. its working organs." Secondly, the machine can not compensate for work-induced physical wear, while the human body, like any living organism, recovers "the worn tissue from its own reserves accumulated during the rest period." Thirdly, he continues, a regular machine is not capable of its own improvement, while the human machine can foster skills by means of exercise. Also, its store of energy and past experience enable human creative actions. It is creativity as a new combination of energy and matter in our world that promotes the progress of human society. This is why the value of man cannot ever be compared to that of technology. Bekhterev believed that the underestimating of this value was the main sin of Taylor's theory.

In defending the idea of the "human machine" as something unique, Bekhterev argued that it should be used in manufacturing as rationally and carefully as possible "in order to reach maximum productivity without harming the physical health and key moral interests of the workers." The Academician insisted that this requirement must be the cornerstone of industrial management at all enterprises, be they private or state-owned. **Any owner must recognize "the special value of a working person."** These remarkable words said at a learned meeting were in fact addressed to Bolsheviks who easily destroyed millions of human lives in the name of their "great" Communist idea that Bekhterev regarded with much skepticism. In another presentation at the conference he said that however we "communize" society, it is unreasonable and impossible to force everybody to act alike under the "turn right and turn left" commands.[165]

If we are indeed moving to socialism we cannot accept that workers who used to toil for capitalists "like beasts of burden" "wasting their muscles, hearts and brains" would now work just as hard for the state. Otherwise it would just mean that a freed slave of individual businessmen becomes a slave to the state. Bekhterev wisely notes that in the long-term the state in this case would gain nothing, since slave labor, as evidenced by many centuries of experience, is always less productive than the labor of free men who are interested in the fruit of their work. He warned that the state thoughtlessly exploiting the energy of its citizens would secure a *temporary* gain in productivity but in the long run would inevitably go into bankruptcy as workers would be getting "overstrained" and "exhausted for a more or less lengthy period of time."[166]

The ultimate ideal in management, according to Bekhterev, would "provide maximum efficiency without exhaustion" and guarantee good health and personal development to the worker. This was the only attitude to scientific management recognized by the famous Russian doctor. He was tirelessly trying to convince the Bolshevik regime that an objective must not be achieved by indiscriminate means, and one must not increase productivity *whatever it takes.*

Bekhterev's ideas of scientific management focused on the issue of *fatigue* and *exhaustion* caused by labor. Of course, he

---

[165] Proceedings of the First All-Russian Initiating NOT Conference ... Vol. 5. Moscow, 1921. P. 57.
[166] Proceedings of the First All-Russian Initiating NOT Conference ... Vol. 1. Moscow, 1921. P. 25.

wrote, any healthy person must work since idleness is bad for the body and may result in its atrophy. Excessive intensification of labor, however, also cannot be tolerated since it leads to overstress and exhaustion. Therefore scientific management should concentrate on precise methods to evaluate muscular and nervous fatigue, the duration of fatigue and the length of rest periods than enable the body to recover and restore its energy.

Bekhterev also found that the worker's *disposition* is an important factor in labor and work motions. For instance, his laboratory found that a joyful mood strengthened pulling motions and weakened bending ones. A depressed mood had an opposite effect. The laboratory also succeeded in identifying the impact of mood on the precision of reproduction that always improved when the worker was in a good mood and vice versa.

Bekhterev and his team conducted extensive research into issues like the position of the body, hands and feet while performing a specific task; coordination and optimization of work motions; the mechanics of muscular contractions; the identification and elimination of the so called unnecessary motions and more. In this work they relied on a simple yet brilliant thought suggested by Taylor who noticed that perhaps forty, fifty, or a hundred ways of doing each act in each trade exist, but there is always one method which is quicker and better than any other.

Bekhterev and his colleagues also studied labor efficiency as a function of nutrition, alcohol, coffee, sleep, ambient temperature, ventilation, lighting and other factors that Taylor just had no time to investigate.

Apart from the physiology of labor, the scholar carried out research into **psychological factors** such as *concentration* (lack of concentration decreases productivity), or *teamwork* (which benefits productivity because collective efforts "have something uplifting and viral about them that makes non-creative team work more productive than individual work.") The **esthetic** aspects of scientific management, according to Bekhterev, have "a valuable effect on the surge of human energy. A bright and attractive interior pleases and cheers up the worker so his productivity increases." Other esthetic factors such as nice music, flowers, paintings, wall coloring have a similar effect. "This is why, - Bekhterev concluded, - industrial premises should be decorated with esthetic principles in mind... We should generally aspire to turn factories and workplaces into something pleasant for the worker, as a good school is for its students."[167]

Finally, Bekhterev had remarkable thoughts on *interest in labor* as a key productivity factor. Research in his laboratory clearly demonstrated that an enthusiastic worker is noticeably more productive than his disinterested counterpart who gets tired much sooner. As a psychophysiologist, Bekhterev explained this finding by observing that interest is a mimico-somatic reflex of a stenic nature that manifests in a greater heart activity, expansion of blood vessels, the rush of arterial blood to working organs and hence a more active metabolism that triggers the defensive reflex against fatigue and over-fatigue. In other words, "interest means higher resistance to fatigue." Therefore, he concluded, "cultivation of interest in work is the best means of raising labor productivity", making labor truly efficient and creative.

How can this interest in labor be cultivated, then? In Bekhterev's works on this arguably *central* problem of scientific management he came up with some valuable thoughts of a political and economic nature. One has to wonder that a medical doctor proved to be more astute than most professional Soviet economists and politicians headed by Lenin. In particular, it was widely believed, as Lenin put it, that socialism would give rise to radical changes in human mentality so people would not be guided solely by economic incentives any more. Bekhterev strongly disagreed. Even before the end of the "war communism" policy that relied on this mesmerizing dogma, he wrote that "whatever we say about the

---

[167] Ibid. P. 33.

moral importance of labor, however we praise its dignity and high social significance [...] *it would be impossible without personal incentives.*"[168]

Bekhterev clearly distinguished between economic and ideological incentives. He perfectly realized that a common worker is not in the least "inclined to be guided by social rather than personal needs because the modern man [...] is an individualist, not a socialist, except, of course, those who have completely assimilated Communist ideas." These people, however, account for a rather small proportion of population that organizes the notorious *subbotniks* and so on. The vast majority may at best experience a temporary surge of enthusiasm instead of a permanent need to subdue to collective interest. Developing economic incentives, therefore, is the key task of scientific management.

While emphasizing he leading role of economic incentives even with the advent of socialism, Bekhterev did not belittle the significance of ideological motives that take their power from a higher source. "They cannot be bought for money, since they have nothing to do with wealth, as we see from the examples of selfless heroism; for moral incentives to work, however, people have to attain a level of culture sufficient for understanding and sharing the ideals of society."[169]

Last, but not least, Bekhterev said we should never ignore such a key factor as the *management system* that must sustain "coordination among all the parts of the production mechanism". He continued that such a function calls for managers who, apart from their professional skills, realize that the interests and health of workers in new Russia are just as important as the business itself.

I could probably write much more about the philosophy of the famous Russian scholar V.V. Bekhterev but what has already

---

[168] Ibid. P. 25.
[169] Ibid. P. 34.

been said is enough to illustrate the significance and originality of his scientific management concepts.

(14) Yermansky Osip Arkadievich (1866 - 1941) - one of the leading pioneers of the Russian labor science, professor, author of the "physiological optimum" concept. His political views were close to Menshevism, although officially he left the Menshevik Party in 1921

Yermansky's political position inspired ferocious criticism from Communist NOT scholars that probably was a major reason why this once popular figure was forgotten. At present it is mentioned rarely, even in the special literature, and usually in a negative context.

This furious criticism was initiated by Lenin who reviewed Yermansky's book "Scientific organization of labor and the Taylor system" (Gosizdat, 1922) in a scathing article "A fly in the ointment." [170] In his typical style ("on the one hand, the book could be a textbook, but on the other hand, it cannot..."), Lenin, although welcoming this publication, claimed it was useless because of the "fly in the ointment" such as the author's "loquacity".

It seems the true meaning of Lenin's review cannot be fully grasped without considering a rather "spicy" episode involving him and Yermansky back in the beginning of the XX century at the Stockholm Joint Congress of the Russian Social-Democratic Labor Party (RSDLP). Votes cast in the election of the Presidium of the Congress turned out to be split equally between the two. In the runoff Yermansky saved Lenin's appointment by refusing to vote for himself. Lenin did cast his ballot for himself and won the race with 60 votes vs. 58 votes for Yermansky. [171] Apparently, the leader had

---

[170] Lenin V.I. Complete Collected Works. V.45. P. 206-207.
[171] Yermansky O.A. Memoirs. [Iz perezhitogo]. M. L., 1927. P. 6.

never forgiven the rival his popularity that was comparable to Lenin's own.

Let us starting our discussion of Yermansky's concept by noting that he was among the first Russian scholars who undertook a deep critical analysis of Western scientific management theories, primary the Taylor system. Suffice it to say that his "Scientific organization of work and the Taylor system" was reprinted four times in Russia and translated in several other countries, including Germany.

According to Yermansky, who shared Bekhterev's views, Taylorism clearly has positive and negative aspects that are "in flagrant antagonism" with each other. The positive part, or the front side of the coin contains the principles of truly scientific organization, whereas the negative part contradicts them completely. This is why, Yermansky maintained, scientific management in general cannot be reasonably equated with Taylorism. Unfortunately, the author continued, such equation is typical of many Russian scientific management scholars fascinated with Taylor's principles.

What is the right vantage point to impartially assess Taylor's system? Yermansky thought that such an assessment required drawing a border between the two main qualities of labor, namely *productivity* and *intensity*. [172]

Yermansky bet on the first quality as the only key to the bright future of scientific management and "a more vibrant and profitable industry." Humanity owns all its progress, he noted, "to increased productivity, improved technologies and innovation aimed at the highest output possible with the least effort."

---

[172] Yermansky O.A. Positive and Negative Aspects of Taylorism. [Polozhitelnye i otritsatelnye storony teylorizma.] Proceedings of the First All-Russian Initiating NOT Conference ... Vol. 1. Moscow, 1921. P. 65.

Labor intensity is another matter. While certainly leading to "the highest output possible," it takes little advantage of new means of production and better management. Rather, its effect is due only to the increase in "the *amount* of energy spent on work in an *unchanged technological environment,*" i.e. due to more **strenuous** work. "This means a higher output is achieved with more rather than less effort." [173]

According to Yermansky, the Taylor system cannot be properly judged without a clear distinction between productivity and the intensity of labor. Namely, anything meant to increase productivity is good and, conversely, whatever methods designed to make labor more intensive (to "squeeze" as much energy from workers as possible) are bad. Once Yermansky formulates this criterion he proceeds to a detailed analysis of the positive and the negative sides of Taylorism.

On the bright side, the Taylor system is designed to achieve the best results with the least expenditure of energy and materials. The actual application of this principle, however, is thwarted by the dark side of that same system.

For instance, the very first pillar of Taylor's system is the notorious "task". In fact, this "task" should be based on a careful study of each trade, each operation and technique invoking physiology, psychotechnics, reflexology and other disciplines. As for Taylor, he determines it using utterly non-scientific means. Time and motion studies, for example, can only record the length and duration of an operation or a motion but involve no analysis.

What does it mean to "analyze" a motion? Yermansky's answer is "to reveal the interdependence among the elements of a complex phenomenon." The stopwatch cannot do this. Time studies involving large numbers of workmen help select the *fastest speed* of the entire operation and make it *mandatory for all workers.* This,

---

[173] Ibid.

however, "is nothing else but mere intensification of labor that has little to do with the analysis aimed at streamlining work motions." Yermansky approvingly quoted Frey who said Taylorism was a way of robbing the worker of his energy to the last ounce without any regard to fatigue. No wonder, he adds, that in each of his books Taylor holds that time studies should involve "the strongest, first-class workmen."

Taylor never cared to ask himself *whether the output prescribed by his system is compatible with physiological limits.* Meanwhile, Yermansky's calculations (willingly or not, he writes nothing about the methodology used, which makes these results questionable) indicate that Schmidt, the famous Taylor's pig iron handler, spent 837,000 kilogram-meters of energy a day instead of the normal 127,000 or the maximum permissible 260,000! "What we are facing here, - Yermansky exclaimed, - is the predatory spending or workmen's energy. It is generally typical for Taylor to take care of saving on the use of *dead matter* such as machinery and implements to achieve the *highest* results with *minimum* spending. When it comes to the *live workforce,* however, Taylor is all into *excessive* energy spending." [174]

Following Yermansky's reasoning we may note that the author is generally right about the bright and the dark sides of Taylor's system but his assessment of these two sides is highly asymmetric. While he obviously belittles the positive aspects of the system, his criticism of the negative aspects is an even more obvious case of overkill. On the other hand, it is exactly this overkill that earned Yermansky many a flattering word from Lenin in the above-mentioned review as the "ointment."

Now let us see what Yermansky had to offer instead of Taylorism that he so strongly recommended not to confuse with the "scientific organization of labor."

---

[174] Ibid. P. 68-69.

I must say that Yermansky, much like Taylor whom he criticized, interpreted the idea of "scientific organization" in a broad way. In his opinion it covers *all* factors of production: machines and implements, their appropriate placement and use, technological processes and their improvement, the live workforce and its sound use, as well as the administration system. [175] Yermansky never challenged the idea of human labor as a *declining factor of production* due to the steady growth in the technical and organic composition of capital, yet strongly believed labor to remain *the backbone of industrial life.* Machines and instruments, however perfect, are still created by man. Since they make physical work easier but cause ever-increasing stress and demand a greater intellectual effort, they demand a higher quality workforce where each man "should be not only a conscious "cog" of his industrial enterprise, but also a conscious contributor in economic development and public life at large." [176]

As we see, Yermansky's concept of various factors subject to "scientific organization" does not differ much from Taylor's. However, Yermansky gives unconditional priority to the human factor. If Taylor's workman is just a "cog" in the giant flywheel of the enterprise who blindly obeys his instruction card, Yermansky thinks of the workman as a "conscious cog" and, moreover, an active contributor to production and public life.

Hence, in contrast to Taylor, Yermansky thought that scientific management must first and foremost maintain the high quality of the workforce and guarantee its sound (as opposed to "predatory") use without any "over-fatigue and exhaustion" whatsoever. Yermansky stressed it was the paramount question of "whether scientific organization of labor should exist at all."

---

[175] Yermansky O.A. Work and Rest. The Problem of Fatigue. [Trud i otdykh. Problema ustalosti.] Proceedings of the First All-Russian Initiating NOT Conference ... Vol. 1. Moscow, 1921. P. 34 -35.
[176] Ibid. P. 35.

Yermansky was amazed that Taylor and his associates dismissed the physiological laws of work and bewildered with the obvious fact that "the four kinds of material energy - mechanical, thermal, electrical and chemical - are the subject of continuous studies, while human energy used in manufacturing has been ill-researched to this day."

Yermansky thinks this is deeply wrong. Problems such as fatigue, exhaustion or rest must be central to scientific management. Russian NOT, he argues, faces a key challenge, that is, it needs to devise a method of measuring fatigue and exhaustion, take control of relevant psychophysiological processes and introduce, *instead of the Taylor system, some truly scientific organization of labor* that would be alien to unsustainable intensification.

Yermansky's reasoning about the fundamentals of scientific organization of labor is also of interest. While defining scientific management as the theory of the best or optimal use of all kinds of energy and all factors of production, Yermansky identified its three basic principles or laws:

1. The law of the organizational sum;
2. The principle of positive selection;
3. The optimum principle.

The first law, originally suggested by A.A. Bogdanov rather than Yermansky, is that an organizational sum exceeds the arithmetic sum of its components.

This becomes possible only if all the material and human elements of production agree with each other in accordance with the positive selection principle. In industry this means selecting the most appropriate implements (in terms of design, weight and shape) and the most appropriate man (in terms of character and physical fitness) for a particular job.

222

However, these two principles, according to Yermansky, are subordinate to the overarching **optimum principle.** [177]

The physiological optimum is the core of Yermansky's concept. He can be credited with raising a crucial and still important issue concerning the proper criteria of sound organization of work that he believed was the principal question of scientific management theory.

The duration or speed of an operation determines the intensity of effort, he argued, but could not be used as such a criterion. Otherwise no limits ought to be set to speed (intensity) while in fact it is curbed by the physical abilities of man. He also rejected the criterion of space, since sometimes the working organ has to cover a longer distance for greater efficiency. While rejecting time and space as criteria for sound organization, he rather regards them as "the forms taken by the phenomena of existence" including manufacturing activities.

He thought the principal elements of any manufacturing activity are the energy expended by all factors of production (E) and the useful result (R) achieved by spending this amount of energy. "An arrangement that leads to a maximum R at the expense of enormous energy consumption is obviously anything but efficient." On the other hand, the least amount of energy spent also cannot be a criterion since in this case the result may be negligible.

What, then, can apply as the only criterion of management efficiency? Yermansky thought it was the ratio between R and E that he calls the efficiency factor or *m*:

m = R / E

---

[177] For more details see: Yermansky O.A. On the criterion of efficiency. [O kriterii ratsionalnosti]. "Za ratsionalizatsiyu", 1928, No.2.

The value m that shows the amount of useful work per unit of energy spent is the best criterion of efficiency. Managers should always strive for the greatest output possible per unit energy or for spending as little energy as possible per unit output. This is the essence of the optimum principle that Yermansky believed to be the cornerstone of NOT. Any violation of this principle means that management is non-scientific since it leads to either squandering all kinds of energy or their underutilization. To achieve the greatest cost-effectiveness one needs in-depth knowledge of manufacturing processes and their human and material factors in order to combine and use them in the most efficient fashion. Apart from this, one certainly needs to know the basic rules of management and the optimum principle itself.

This is the essence of Yermansky's concept that was fiercely yet sometimes rather pointlessly criticized by his peers. Contrary to Yermansky's high expectations, it never became universally recognized[178]. Its main highlight, in our view, is the idea of the need to maintain productivity at an optimal, evidence-based level, since deviations from the sensible norm to either side are "extremely harmful in terms of the national economy and the sound use of all resources."[179] Accordingly, the management system must ensure the normal operation of all departments and all employees.

However, this concept was not without major flaws. As A.K. Gastev noted, the author largely ignored the challenges faced by the Russian economy in the 1920s after it was all but shattered by the revolution and the war. Enormous efforts were needed to recover the economy on an advanced technological basis as soon as possible. Yermansky's concept in this context sounded way too idealistic. Many points he made (e.g. the need to measure energy consumption by monitoring the amount of oxygen inhaled and

---

[178] Yermansky O.A. Theory and practice of innovation. *[Teoriya i praktika ratsionalizatsii]* Moscow-Leningrad, 1925. P. XI.
[179] Yermansky O.A. The criterion of rationality. *[O kriterii ratsionalnosti.]* P. 7.

carbon dioxide exhaled by the worker, as well as some others) seemed pretty Utopian.

Yermansky also vastly exaggerated the universal significance of the optimum principle, claiming it to be the sole core of scientific management. In terms of methodology, this absolutization was not very compatible with the comprehensive approach supported by Yermansky. He also acted in a highly intolerant way. In particular, he strongly criticized Gastev's "narrow base" concept as "primitive" and improperly castigated Vitke's nascent socio-psychological analysis of management.

Again, however, no critical analysis of Yermansky's concepts should overshadow their undisputed value. His message to modern economists is that they should look for management and production arrangements that neither overstress nor underuse the workman so as to eventually ensure sustained productivity growth.

(15) Strumilin (Strumillo-Petrashkevich) Stanislav Gustavovich (1877 - 1974) – an eminent Soviet economist and statistician, member of the USSR Academy of Sciences. He wrote over 700 papers in the field of economics, statistics, management, demography, political economy and economic history. Strumilin stood at the origins of Soviet economic planning as one of the leading developers of the first five-year plans. He also directed the development of the first ever stock management system for raw materials. Winner of the Lenin Prize (1958) and the State Prize (1942).

(16) Bogdanov, Aleksandr Aleksandrovich (1873 - 1928) – an outstanding economist, philosopher, natural scientist, physician, writer and professor of Moscow State University. Bogdanov could break new ground in any theoretical of practical area touched by his powerful intellect. For instance, in his medical capacity he was the founder and head of the world's first Institute of Blood Transfusion. While strictly forbidding his staff to conduct risky blood transfusion experiments on themselves, he made the only exception for himself. The twelfth experiment proved fatal.

Our project includes a separate book on this outstanding person. Nevertheless, let us dwell briefly on his exceptional contribution to Russian scientific management. His principal brainchild was a concept he called **tectology,** or **the universal organization science.**

Bogdanov believed the issue of organization included three components, that is, things, people and ideas, and could not be handled by means of historical wisdom or organizational talents alone. He endeavored to systematize the enormous organizational experience of humanity and equip leaders with the knowledge of the relevant laws. He also maintained that the art of organization had always existed, in contrast to the science of organization. Therefore most achievements in management died with the achiever, a talent or a genius, and just a tiny fraction of them survived by turning into a tradition.

What should be the subject of organization science? According to Bogdanov, it should study general principles and laws that govern processes of organization in all areas of organic and inorganic world: physical and psychological phenomena in life and nature, in the impact of elemental forces and in conscious human activity. [180] He argued that these laws exist in technology (organization of things), the economy (organization of people) and ideology (organization of ideas). Thus, "the paths of nature's spontaneous creativity as well as the ways of conscious human organizational activity can and must be subject to scientific analysis." Until now, Bogdanov noted, these paths and methods had not been precisely identified for the lack of a universal organization science, "whose time has come now." [181]

---

[180] Bogdanov A.A. Essays on the Universal Organizational Science. [Ocherki vseobshchey organizatsionnoy nauki.] Samara, 1921. P.11.
[181] Ibid. P.11.

Bogdanov elaborated the basic concepts and methods of organization science. In particular, he suggested the systems approach for handling organizational issues and interpreted the relation between a system and its components by demonstrating that the organized whole may exceed the simple sum of its parts. [182] How do we explain his paradoxical assertion that a combination of activities may either decrease or increase their practical sum? Well, any activity meets a certain resistance. The whole can be greater than the sum of its parts if the process of organization causes a smaller loss to combined activities than to their combined resistances. Thus, the elements of any organization can be analyzed in terms of activities and resistances. Bogdanov claimed that any system must be analyzed in relation to its environment and to each of its elements. "The first and foremost notions of tectology refer to elements and their combinations. These elements are activities and resistances of all sorts. Combinations may be organized, disorganized and neutral. They the practical sum of their elements may vary." [183]

Bogdanov also suggested a number of revealing thoughts on the structural stability of a system and its factors; the forming and the regulative mechanisms; the need to use mathematics for the analysis of organizations. He put forward the idea of "biregulators" (the dual mechanism of mutual control) similar to the feedback concept in cybernetics, introduced the principle of "chain connection", "the minimum principle" and more.

Bogdanov used his approach to make a daring and exciting attempt to create a monistic concept of the universe. Since he believed that organization was the essence of animate and

---

[182] An average Arab soldier in a one on one clash is no worse than an average French soldier, noted Bogdanov. However, a detachment of 200 French soldiers is in fact stronger than that of an Arab unit of 300-400 men, and a French army of 10 thousand would defeat a local army of 30 to 40 thousand men. (Ibid. P.46).
[183] Ibid. P.48.

inanimate nature, he in fact reduced any activity to organizational activity. In his view, humanity has no other activities besides organizational activities, no other problems, no other points of view on life and the world, except for organizational ones. The universe, Bogdanov argued, acts as an infinitely unfolding tissue of systems that feature different types and levels of organization (complete disorganization simply does not exist – it is a meaningless word). The struggle and interactions among these systems form the universal organizational process. All of these forms in their intertwining and struggle form a global organizational process that can be split into an infinite number of elements yet remains an integral and continuous whole.

What about destructive, i.e. disorganizing activities? Bogdanov admitted to their existence but classified them as a specific kind of organizational activities. "If social classes or groups, - he wrote – clash to disorganize each other, the reason is precisely that each such class or group strives after organizing the world and humanity according to their own needs. These clashes result from the fact that organizing forces are separated and isolated, and have yet to attain a harmonious unity. They are the struggle of organizational forms. "

The two main organizational mechanisms mentioned above are central to Bogdanov's concept.

The forming mechanism includes components such as conjugation (combination of complexes), ingression (when two complexes share an element) and disingression (disintegration of the complex). Let us consider these terms in greater detail.

Human organizational activity in any area, according to Bogdanov, means connecting and separating the available elements. For instance, "labor is nothing but combining various materials, implements and manpower, and removing some of their parts to arrive at the organized whole, i.e. the 'product'." [184] These two acts, the connection and the separation, do not play an equal role in human activity; the former is primary, the latter secondary. The combination of complexes (the primary moment) is the foundation of a tectological mechanism called "conjugation," a term borrowed from biology. Bogdanov's "conjugation" was a sweeping notion that covered partnership or any kind of other communication, alloying metals, exchange of goods between factories and much more (the assimilation of food, hugs and kisses, a meeting of workers, a military skirmish and so on). Complexes can unite (which leads to an organizatonal crisis and makes the tectological border between them disappear) to form a fundamentally different system directly, via "ingression" or the formation of a ligament. A system that consists of complexes connected by a ligament is called an ingressive system. Conjugated systems may also disintegrate into new separate entities with new borders. This process called "disingression" also entails an organizational crisis of the system, though of a different nature. "All crises observed in life and nature, - claimed Bogdanov - all "coups d'etat", "revolutions", "catastrophes" and so on belong to these two types. For example, social revolutions typically break boundaries between classes; boiling water breaks the physical boundary between the liquid and the atmosphere; the reproduction of a living cell gives rise to a border between its newly independent parts and so forth." [185]

In addition to the forming mechanism "tectology" has a regulating mechanism that selects the best combination of elements. Selection, according to Bogdanov, is the only way "forms" can survive in nature. Selection can be positive or negative; it may occur in developing complexes as well as in those suffering a relative decline. These two types of selection collectively cover all natural and social processes, and their complementary unity spontaneously organizes the world.

---

[184] Ibid. P.63.
[185] Ibid. P.75.

Therefore, Bogdanov's organizational model is a universal concept that he applied to an infinite range of processes and phenomena in both nature and society.

Bogdanov wrote that "Man in his organizing activity is only a disciple and imitator of nature as the great universal organizer. Therefore no human method can go beyond the methods of nature and will always be just a particular instance of these methods." [186]

Bogdanov applied the principles of his universal organizational science to economic management and planning, particularly on the national scale. In fact, this was the subject of his presentation at the First All-Russian NOT Conference. The development of a plan, he claimed, critically depends on the understanding of functional chain connections between various sectors and therefore should take into account the tectological "law of the least." In his own words, according to this law "the strength of a chain is determined by the weakest of its links; the speed of a squadron by its slowest vessel; the yield of crops by the factor least favorable to the harvest (Liebig's law of the minimum) and so on. According to this law the rate of economic growth depends on the sectors that lag behind the most." [187]

Bogdanov held that this law applied to physical, mental, social and economic systems alike. If, for example, the output of iron grows by 5%, he wrote, all the industries that depend on it through a chain connection, can only grow by 5% - for otherwise they would be short of iron; and if they grow by less than 5%, a certain part of iron would be redundant. Similarly, industries that supply raw materials and technology for the production of iron must produce 5% more than previously. [188]. This is why economic processes also obey the law of the least.

---

[186]Ibid. P.63.
[187] Bogdanov A.A. Organizational science and economic planning. [Organizatsionnaya nauka i khozyaystvennaya planomernost']. "Proceedings of the First Russian Conference…" V.1. P.12.

Some authors claimed this law implied "alignment with the weakest". We beg to disagree; Bogdanov was obviously right even in terms of common sense. The idea of the "weakest link in the chain" later became the basis of network planning and management that are widely used today in various fields.

Developing this idea elsewhere, Bogdanov suggested some insights concerning the law of least in the area of industrial management. A manager, he wrote, can sustain his the business in a sound way for years by means of shrewd and timely interventions. Yet a single error of judgment or an occasional lack of attention can spell disaster, like in a combat situation. On a more detailed level, that same law is responsible for the inevitable historical limitations of authoritarian organizations that wholly depend on the individual brain of "the boss" or "the sovereign," while the life of an organization is certainly a collective phenomenon. Therefore, just a short-lived small failure of an individual may deal the entire collective a severe and even fatal blow. [189] Needless to say how relevant this idea sounds today.

The reaction to Bogdanov's "tectology" was hostile to say the least. His organizational ideas were fiercely criticized and his very name by the late 20s turned into an ideological stigma. The word "Bogdanovism" was perhaps the most terrible political label to be put on a scholar during "scientific" arguments.

Was there any logic behind this unfortunate and irrational rejection of Bogdanov's organizational science? We believe there were several reasons for that. First of all, Bogdanov's ideas were certainly far ahead of their time. Russian, and, for that matter, global scientific management obviously had not advanced enough to appreciate these ideas even at an elementary level. Similar works by Bertalanffi, Wiener and others were published much later and welcomed by a more prepared scientific community. Secondly,

---

[188] Ibid.
[189] Bogdanov A.A. Essays on the Universal Organizational Science. P. 94-95.

Bogdanov presented his tectology in a highly sophisticated language replete with philosophical vocabulary, as well as specific terminology borrowed from natural sciences, which, of course, did not make it any easier for scientific management scholars and practitioners to grasp his message. Third, the plight of the "universal organization science" was largely affected by Lenin's circumstantial, severe and often unfair criticism of Bogdanov's philosophy in "Materialism and Empiriocriticism." This fact was deftly used by social scientists from the Kremlin in their "analysis" of tectology (incidentally, Lenin never read Bogdanov but just "gave appropriate instructions" to his comrades). Finally, Bogdanov's science was presented to the reader at a difficult time in Russia. The economy collapsed all but completely after World War I, the October Revolution and the policy of "war communism", resources were in short supply and scholars were naturally expected to develop practical guidance on how to spend as little time and resources as possible to boost economic performance. Many in this situation believed there was no need whatsoever for general theoretical concepts. While dealing with specific problems such as the smart organization of the workplace, improvements in the structure of the control system or the simplification of workflow, these scientists, so to say, "overlooked" Bogdanov organizational science. In fact, they failed to realize that a purely pragmatic approach often does not allow "to see the forest for the trees."

It was but several decades later that Bogdanov's principal ideas (the isomorphism between various organizational structures, entropy, feedback and "chain" connections, "the law of the least" and others) resurfaced to be further developed in disciplines such as the general systems theory, cybernetics, the organizational theory or synergetics. The inherent relation of tectology to these sciences is obvious today, and Bogdanov's name now ranks with Bertalaffi, Wiener, Ashby and other equally celebrated names. Western experts agree. John Gorelik, a Canadian professor, calls tectology the first ever detailed version of the general systems theory and a forerunner of cybernetics. [190] Another Canadian

232

professor, R. Mattessich, gives Bogdanov even more credit by claiming that he was the true father of the systems theory rather than Bertalanffy, as is generally believed.[191]

The issues of precedence are certainly important for any national science and deserve more than the often easy-going attitude of Russian scholars. Yet even more important is the fact that Bogdanov's ideas that were burned at the bonfires of the Bolshevik Inquisition, re-emerged like a phoenix from the ashes. Fortunately, such great manuscripts do not burn.

(17) Smith-Falkner, Mariya Natanovna (1878 - 1968) – a renowned Soviet economist, Correspondent Member of the USSR Academy of Sciences. She worked on economic planning, statistics, industrial management and certain general issues of political economy and the history of economics.

(18) Vitke Nikolay Andreyevich (? -?) - an outstanding Russian scholar, a leading organizer of the NOT movement in the country, head of the standardization department at RKI. Unfortunately, we have no information about the dates of his birth and death. Vitke's concept was a new word in Russian as well as global scientific management. This, however, became clear only several decades later. In the 1920s his colleagues overwhelmingly took it as "reactionary nonsense" that had to be refuted. Under the pressure of fierce criticism the scientist was forced to retreat. In the wake of this pseudo-criticism his theory was virtually banned, which doomed Russian scientific management to lag behind the West for half a century. Vitke himself was likely executed or died in prison.

As already mentioned, this remarkable scholar, as well as Gastev and Bogdanov, will be the subject of a separate book. Therefore this note will be brief.

---

[190] Bogdanov A.A, Tectology: A Universal Organization Science. [Tektologiya (Vseobshchaya organizatsionnaya nauka)]. V.1. Moscow, 1989. P.13.
[191] Ibid. P.14.

Vitke, as far as we know, was the first scholar in history who advocated the critical importance of **a social approach** to management. Many of his ideas in fact took precedence over the concept of *human relations* that emerged later in the USA. Only the lack of care for our own history can explain why no one has ever insisted on the Russian priority in this area.

According to Vitke, management essentially means organizing human energy to reach a certain purpose. "A modern administrator, - he explained - is primarily a social engineer or technician (depending on his position in the system), a constructor of human relations." [192] Vitke urged to abandon Taylor's and Ford's view of people engaged in manufacturing as "small cogs in a complex machine." To him, management was all about analyzing and controlling human relations arising in the labor process, creating a system of cooperation and maintaining a favorable social as well as psychological climate at workplace that he called "the spirit of a beehive". "An efficient organization, - he wrote, - requires much more than precise planning of the production process, an ideal distribution of functions or a fully automated control system. It is not possible to foster labor automatism and create a viable production entity against the will of the people, or even in the absence of such will." [193]

This insightful reasoning challenges the entire classical school of management that focused on organizational and technological issues, while largely ignoring the social aspects of management.

Engineering skills are not the main advantage of a strong manager. He should, first and foremost, act as "the leader of human efforts." Vitke provided a description of such an ideal leader who can advance team spirit by encouraging common drive, coordinate

---

[192] Vitke N.A. Management and industrial development. [Organizatsiya upravleniya i industrialnoe razvitie.] Moscow, 1925. P.72.
[193] Ibid. P.77.

the activities of all enterprise units and convince all employees that their work is needed and appreciated. The famous Hawthorne experiments in the late 1920s and early 1930s amply corroborated many of his ideas.

(19) Rudakov, Mikhail Petrovich (? -?) – a well-known Soviet NOT scholar. Gastev's negative attitude to Rudakov appears somewhat biased. Rudakov offered an interesting interpretation of management as a complex *economic* phenomenon. His goal was to improve the fragmented functional approach to management and develop a single concept that would encompass a variety of economic functions and management methods. It was a valuable contribution, since most scholars at the time analyzed management in terms of organization and technology, while the economic dimension of this complex phenomenon was largely ignored.

The aim of economic management, according to Rudakov, is the organization of continuous expanded reproduction, i.e. the proper organization of the production cycle and the capital circulation cycle so that capital would return to the enterprise in the amount sufficient to cover costs and expand production. Rudakov believed that "management relates to profit as a factory relates to its physical output"[194] and directly blamed loss-making on poor management.

The compatibility between government planning and industrial self-financing *(khozraschet)* was also central to Rudakov's concept. These two instruments, he wrote, are the primary means of government control over individual economic agents. Planning, however, unites various elements of the national economy into a single system, whereas self-financing focuses "on management skills of individuals." Both methods are quite autonomous. However, the isolated use of "either planning or self-financing" cannot sustain proper management efficiency.

---

[194] Rudakov M.P. Accounting and planning in management. [Uchetno-planovaya sistema upravleniya.] Moscow, 1924. P. 53.

Rudakov's ideal is a harmonious synthesis of these two methods. How can this be achieved is a major theoretical and practical question. Rudakov's proposed an "accounting and planning system" (APS) that can be briefly described as follows.

Since the principal function of management is the organization of turnover, the latter should be divided into separate components. Each of these, in turn, consists of some subcomponents subject to detailed planning and rigorous accounting and control. In this way all the movement of products and labor in the course of production and turnover may be analyzed to the smallest element and precisely calculated. Rudakov believed this approach would neutralize the human factor in management and turn it into an orderly well-calculated system that would be hardly dependent on managers' intellect and skills. The author proudly described his theory as ""the ABC of mechanization and clear-cut, simple administration." Simplified and mechanized administration, he claimed, was the key to further progress of scientific management.

Rudakov raised a truly important issue of improving economic management in Soviet Russia. It is easy to see, however, that he carried his reasoning to the point of absurdity akin to Lenin's idea that "any kitchen maid should be able to run the state." By reducing all management functions to "simple motions" that ostensibly can be calculated in advance and standardized, he left no room in his system for management art that requires profound general and professional knowledge. He also ignored the fact of emergency situations that need a fast and unconventional response from the manager.

Any further presentation of Rudakov's wordy and occasionally witty deliberations on the ways and means to combine the government-imposed plan with market mechanisms into an integrated "accounting and planning system" would probably tire the reader. He certainly did not realize that his attempts were doomed anyway, as evidenced by the vain persistence of Kremlin's economists over the decades of the Bolshevik regime. Central planning in the long run always suppressed and killed the market.

It would be unfair, however, to judge Rudakov's theory exclusively by its flaws. He can be commended for raising management to the rank of an economic category, calling the attention of economists to management and emphasized the need for a mechanism that would integrate all its separate elements.

(20) This opinion appears somewhat far-fetched. Gastev was certainly fascinated with Lenin whom he regarded as an outstanding person who, incidentally, at some point did help Gastev secure some financing. After their personal meeting Lenin wrote a letter to the People's Commissariat of Finance which read as follows: "I'd really like to help comrade Gastev, head of the Institute of Labor. He needs 0.5 million in gold to buy stuff. Sure we can ill afford this right now... Think about it, and do your best to get him a certain amount."[195] Many statements by Lenin such as "obedience" and "work culture" actually agreed well with Gastev's concepts. But let's face it: to defend himself from numerous opponents Gastev, who was not a member of the Communist Party, was forced to appeal to Lenin's authority and seek ideological endorsement in his works that, as is well-known, always left plenty of room for ambiguous interpretations. So Gastev literally "pecked out" the sympathetic ideas he needed and ignored others that often had an opposite meaning and were gladly used by TsIT's foes.

(21) Isaak Naftulovich Shpilreyn was widely known in the NOT community. Head of the Industrial Psychotechnics Laboratory under the People's Commissariat of Labor, he was one of the leading experts in the psychotechical area of scientific management. Among his numerous works are "Psychotechnics and professional orientation: Summary of a course." (Moscow, 1924), "Professional

---

[195] Lenin V.I. Collected works (in Russian). V. 52. P. 244-245.

selection: methods and achievements" (Moscow-Leningrad, 1925), "On the theory of psychotechnics" (Moscow, 1931).

Shpilreyn held that psychotechnics should cover a broad range of issues. The principal one, however, was the determination of professional fitness as a means of successful management.

Modern society, he wrote, is dominated by the ever-deepening division of labor, with hundreds of occupations and thousands of narrow professions. Each trade calls for specific human qualities such as great physical strength, dexterity, faultless eye, long-term attention, good memory for numbers, fast response and so on. Many professions require a combination of two or more qualities. Clearly, to be fit for a particular trade one should possess appropriate physical and mental abilities. The national economy can operate at a peak capacity only if as many workers as possible are employed according to their particular talents. In real life, he notes, this is not the case; moreover, managers frequently complain about the shortage of proper personnel and the poor quality of work done by unfit people. And, of course, good workers are appreciated anywhere.

The two-prong task of psychotechnics, according to Shpilreyn, is (1) to identify and classify the requirements of various professions, and (2) to develop a methodology of matching people to appropriate jobs.

At the final stage of a psychotechnical test individual abilities are compared to requirements for various professions and recommendations are made as follows: 1) professions most suitable for the tested person; 2) professions that are suitable for him or her with reservations; and 3) professions that are not suitable at all. Such recommendations should always take into account the economic aspects of employment such as the current demand for this particular profession, wages, length and cost of education and so on.

In addition to the general theoretical results, Shpilreyn devised many original tests and provided a detailed description of requirements for a range of professions, thus making a distinct contribution to Russian scientific management.

(22) Burdyansky, Iosif Mendelevich (1895 - 1937) – a well-known figure of the NOT movement in Russia, the founder and director of the Kazan Institute of Scientific Organization of Labor (KINOT), professor.

Burdyansky used his own version of the functional approach to scientific management. First, his always customized his analysis in accordance with the economy, sector or factory-specific features of management. Secondly, he was also interested in the theory of management and its differences from other human activities.

In particular, Burdyansky rejected a popular assumption that reduced management to a purely technological process. He maintained: "Since management covers a range of specific functions (accounting, planning, control, cost calculations and so on) that cannot be handled by technology... we have to admit that management is an activity that does not depend on technology alone."[196] Moreover, he correctly notes that technological activities in industry also have to be managed.

Burdyansky assumed that scientific management has the following principal functions:
   1) work preparation and planning in space and time;
   2) all types of accounting;
   3) monitoring of implementation;
   4) organization of research.

These functions are separate from each other. Burdyansky, however, added a complementary function, that of *coordination* or

---

[196] Burdyansky I.M. Innovation and technology. [Ratsionalizatsiya i tekhnika]. "Problemy ekonomiki", 1929, No.7-8. P. 193.

leadership to tie all the other functions together. Therefore he became was one of the first Russian scholars to identify a function that unites various areas of management and turns it into an integrated phenomenon.

Burdyansky left several insightful thoughts on scientific management. As early as in 1921 he claimed that management should become an independent science with its own area of research.[197] Somewhat later, he challenged the idea that management was only an art that relied solely on the innate talent of the administrator. "Needless to say that talent is a good thing, but good management of an enterprise or an institution requires special knowledge, just as driving a locomotive requires knowledge of the machine."[198] Management has its own laws and should be studied by a stand-alone science, since certain management-specific issues are not covered by other disciplines. He probably just had a feeling that such issues existed and never identified them concretely. In the 1960s, however, the Management Research Centre at the Department of Economics of Moscow State University and Moscow Management University further developed this idea and applied it to practice.

Burdyansky viewed applied research as a key area of industrial management. He maintained that any factory needs, apart from accounting, control and planning departments, a special research unit dealing with improvements in production and management as well as practical innovation. In fact, as noted above, in the second half of the 1920 such units (factory laboratories or practical innovation departments) were increasingly replacing pilot stations and orga-stations.

However, by the end of the 1920s, opposition to the very existence of special industrial innovation units mounted in the

---

[197] Burdyansky I.M. Scientific organization of labor. [Nauchnaya organizatsiya truda.] Leningrad, 1925. P. 58.
[198] Ibid.

literature as well as at the top of the government. In the 1930s all of them, including RKI, were shut down. Oddly enough, Burdyansky, who had so recently defended these bodies, played a key role in their liquidation. He explained that such research units designed to make specific recommendations to improve production and management were needed when scientific management was in its infancy and just a handful of people was aware of its principles and methods. As socialist industry advances, however, and more and more people are involved in innovation and improvement, research and innovation are bound to disappear as a distinct area of the manufacturing process. Therefore no special innovation units will be needed anymore.[199] Global experience demonstrates that Burdyansky was fundamentally wrong on this issue.

We regret to note that Burdyansky often resorted to rather obscene methods of discussion with his opponents (including Gastev) by sending denunciations to the secret police. This did not help him to survive, however; in 1937 he was executed.

(23) Radus-Zenkovich, Viktor Alekseevich (1877 - 1967) – a politician, a statesman and a revolutionary. In matters of NOT he was lending active support to P.M. Kerzhentsev and participated in the creation of the Time League.

(24) Kerzhentsev Platon Mikhailovich (1881 - 1940) - a well-known politician and statesman, economist, historian and writer. He was the Russian ambassador to Sweden and Italy, worked as Deputy Manager of the Central Statistical Agency and as the chief censor in the country. He also held prominent positions in the NOT movement such as a member of the Presidium of the All-Union NOT Council at CCC-RKI and Chairman of the Time League. Kerzhentsev published numerous works on scientific management such as "Principles of Organization" (Selected Works. Moscow, 1968); "Struggle for time" (Moscow, 1965), "Organize yourself" (Moscow-

---

[199] Burdyansky I.M. Innovation and technology. [Ratsionalizatsiya i tekhnika]... P. 191-202.

Leningrad, 1927) and "NOT: Scientific organization of labor and tasks of the Party"(Moscow-Petrograd, 1923).

Kerzhentsev supported Bogdanov's idea that all the various forms of organization in nature, technology and society share some common features and principles for a special science to study; his approach, however, was limited to *management processes in society,* or *in human groups regardless of their activities.* Kerzhentsev believed that scientific laws apply to any type of management. Appropriate organization, he wrote, must become the cornerstone of society including not only some enterprises or industries but also the entire economy, government, the army, trade-unions and the Party, in other words, to all entities in the country. As you can see, Kerzhentsev's methodology remains broad enough despite its limitations. His idea that any organizational work with people follows some general laws essentially anticipated the main principle of *praxeology* with regard to management. This approach led him to a valuable idea that management experience can be transplanted from one area to another, e.g. "military experience can be somehow used in industry, industrial management practices can be used in cultural work and so on." [200]

Kerzhentsev formulated a number of general principles for an efficient organization that needs, in particular, to set its goals and objectives, to select a structure, develop a plan and a work methodology, set a policy of using physical and human resources and establish accounting and control mechanisms.

Unfortunately, Kerzhentsev was a pure Kremlin ideologist never tired of "proving" that NOT has no future under capitalism as opposed to its boundless potential in a socialist state. Accordingly, Gastev rightly criticized his quest for "philosophers' stone, i.e. the Communist NOT".

---

[200] Kerzhentsev P.M. NOT. Moscow-Petrograd. 1923. P. 54.

(25) A few words about the Time League that was established by P.M. Kerzhentsev, who became its chairman. According to Kerzhentsev, no scientific management could develop without such an association. Tangible results, he wrote, can be expected only "if we stimulate interest in NOT in broad working masses and engage them in active NOT work." [201] Of course, the author continued, the development of scientific management does need research institutes and laboratories, but equally needed are mass organizations to support and enhance research and development.

Established in 1923, the Time League quickly expanded its ranks to tens of thousands of members across the country and effectively became the grassroots wing of the NOT movement. Later it was renamed the NOT League whose founders, apart from Kerzhentsev, included I.N. Shpilreyn, I.A. Zalkind, M.P. Rudakov and A.M. Kaktyn.[202]

(26) Goltsman, Abram Zinovievich (1894 - 1933) – a well-known economist and statesman, a loyal and reliable ally of Gastev whom he joined as a co-signer of "The Platform of Four." Goltsman took an active part in the restructuring of RKI. His works include, in particular, "Reorganization of man" (Leningrad, 1925); "The organization of labor in the USSR" (Moscow, 1925) and "Industrial management in Germany and in the USSR" (Moscow-Leningrad, 1930).

In contrast to Kerzhentsev, Goltsman supported Gastev's belief that the accomplishments of Western scientific management need not be treated with "Communist arrogance" and Russia should not waste time and money on re-discovering ideas long familiar to the capitalist world. Quite the opposite, he wrote, we must fully use capitalist industrial experience as soon as possible, transfer all their

---

[201] Kerzhentsev P.M. NOT at the economic front. [*NOT na khozyaystvennom fronte.*] "Vremya", 1924, No.4. P. 4.

[202] Kerzhentsev P.M. Principles of organization. [*Printsipy organizatsii*]. Moscow, 1968. P. 453.

best practices to Soviet industry and master all their achievements to proceed at an ever faster pace."[203]

Goltsman was a keen organizer of the NOT movement in Russia. He believed it was indispensable in a situation where most enterprises "still wallow in the swamp of purely Russian technological and cultural backwardness"[204] In those grim days Goltsman came up with interesting and bold ideas on economic methods of management, primarily self-financing of public enterprises, at a time when the essentially opposite "administrative command" approach was on the rise. He had to pay the price for his views almost immediately, as early as in 1933.

(27) Rozmirovich Elena Fedorovna (1885 - 1953) - a major figure of the NOT movement in the USSR, the founder and director of the country's first specialized Institute of Management Technology under CCC-RKI (IMT).

Rozmirovich developed a distinct concept called "the industrial interpretation of management" based on the idea of similarity between manufacturing and management processes (originally put forward, as we remember, by Gastev). First, Rozmirovich claimed, these processes consist of the same elements. Secondly, manufacturing and managements follow the same principles. [205]

The director of IMT suggested that the structure of physical labor (e.g. manufacturing) and that of intellectual labor such as management (e.g. drafting a plan or a corporate balance sheet) share many fundamental features. She defined management as "a purely technical process of coordinating and organizing the use of workforce in industry or administration that is carried out by a

---

[203] Goltsman A.Z. Industrial management in Europe and in the USSR. [*Upravlenie promyshlennostyu v Germanii i v SSSR.*] Moscow, 1930. P. 9.
[204] Goltsman A.Z. At the threshold of innovation. [*U poroga ratsionalizatsii.*] "Khozyaistvo i upravlenie", 1926, No.3. P. 13.
[205] The State Institute of Management Technology. [*Gosudarstvennyy institut tekhniki upravleniya.*] Moscow, 1928. P. 7.

certain category of people with the help of special techniques applied to groups of individuals or things." [206] She believed that management as an array of planning, supervisory, controlling and regulatory (in a broad sense) actions does not substantially differ from the manufacturing process.

This basic principle of "industrial interpretation" *stemmed from a peculiar concept of management.* Rozmirovich thought that any management unit may be regarded as a complex machine, or system of machines engaged in a production process "expressed physically in artifacts such as folders, orders, recorded telephone message, cards, files and so on." [207]

She further reasoned that research into industrial labor and the elimination of needless motions make it possible to improve and automate the manufacturing process that increasingly uses sophisticated machines organized in large systems. Accordingly, the work of machine operators boils down to a number of simple motions to control the machine. Since management is similar to manufacturing, its elements may likewise be planned and streamlined. One can break management down into individual operations, study their sequence and measure them in time and space, just as Gastev's school recommended with regard to the "management of things". The management process can thus be calculated in advance and automated. Note that Rozmirovich applied this principle to all levels of management, from a factory to the entire country.

Thus, the mechanization of production suggested that of management, whose functions would be reduced to simple motions. By assuming that all actions of a manager ("motions") can be calculated and standardized in advance, Rozmirovich left no room for any creativity. Moreover, she elaborated her position by

---

[206] Rozmirovich E. NOT, RKI and the Party. [*NOT, RKI i partiya.*] Moscow, 1926. P. 209.
[207] Ibid. P. 160-161.

arguing that mechanization, once mature, will make managerial work redundant, since "machines themselves will already control the worker on their own," while management would be reduced to formal supervision and automatic control and therefore would cease to be a special authoritative function. She maintained that "the system of managing people" should be replaced by "the system of managing things", and management functions would "gradually lose their authority" and finally disappear altogether, as "special functions of a special kind of people." [208] The social aspect of management would be steadily declining and "nothing would be left for the administration and management ... of the team. Here we deal with the **omnipotence** of technology that turns the administrator into nothing more than a technician."[209]

As we see, this ideology offers a rather bleak future to management that will presumable disappear as "a special function of a special kind of people."

Note, however, that despite these pessimistic forecasts Rozmirovich herself made a significant contribution to certain areas of applied scientific management such as the problem of management structures, functions and principles, as well as the means of improving management.

The "industrial interpretation" emerged during the period of NEP-induced fast recovery of the economy shattered by the war, the revolution and the "war communism", when it was becoming clear that the next (reconstructive) stage of economic growth would demand uncompromising austerity.

How can management be made as inexpensive and simple as possible? What are the ways to streamline administrative processes

---

[208] Rozmirovich E. Towards better state governance. [*Osnovnye polozheniya po ratsionalizatsii apparata gosudarstvennogo upravleniya.*] "Tekhnika upravleniya", 1926, No.7. P. 14.
[209] Rozmirovich E. NOT, RKI and the Party. [*NOT, RKI i partiya.*] Moscow, 1926. P. 185.

to ensure the highest return? Rozmirovich believed **the use of technology** was the answer. Indeed, management involves a complex network of various components and can be studied in various contexts such as economics, law, sociology or psychology. The technological component also plays a role, so, once again, research into the technological aspects of management is perfectly legitimate.

Relying on the assumed similarity between production and management processes, Rozmirovich, like Gastev, somewhat anticipated the fundamental ideas of cybernetics, the systems theory and other disciplines. It was only natural for her to advocate streamlining and automation as the means to address management issues. *Some other principles and assumptions of the "industrial" interpretation*, however, seem rather problematic. Indeed, Rozmirovich had **a fundamentally wrong answer** to two key methodological questions.

1. Is it possible to simplify management to such an extent that it could be mastered by most people like regular low-skilled trades or, in the long run, by any worker? Do we need any professionally trained managers? Can management be organized in such a way as to possibly involve simple and often semi-illiterate peasants or machine operators?
2. Can the technological approach to management be declared the only one valid, while others would be proclaimed false and unscientific?

Let's start with the first question. As a loyal disciple of Lenin, Rozmirovich blindly professed Bolshevik ideas and was fanatically devoted to the letter and spirit of Leninism. Hence her affirmative response to this question was an evident fallacy.

Recall Lenin's "The State and Revolution": *"All* citizens becomes employees and workers of a *single* countrywide state "syndicate". All that is required is that they should work equally, do their proper share of work, and get equal pay; the accounting and control necessary for this have been *simplified* by capitalism to the utmost and reduced to the extraordinarily simple operations--which any literate person can perform--of supervising and recording, knowledge of the four rules of arithmetic, and issuing appropriate receipts." [210]

These days, after so many disasters and absurdities, it is easy to see and appreciate that such simple prescriptions are fatal to the economy and management. In the 1920s, however, this seductive easiness quickly won the hearts and minds of the masses, was picked up by many economists and rapidly replicated in hundreds and thousands of articles, collections and monographs to become the main paradigm of socialist management. In the long run, of course, the idea of steady "simplification" of management functions was a spectacular failure.

Consider the second question. Can the technological approach to management be declared the only one valid, while others would be proclaimed false and unscientific? Certainly not. This extreme approach ignores the distinctly social nature of management. Rozmirovich reduced manufacturing to technology and denied management any special features. Hence her hasty conclusion that management could also be treated in terms of technology. The above-mentioned false premise was bringing about new delusions.

While running to extremes, the director of IMT tried to prove there was no social aspect in management. Since this was impossible without sinning against the truth, however, Rozmirovich went to the next step by admitting the social dimension of management and the need to control groups of people, but only under capitalism, that ostensibly had to crush the workers' class resistance using a variety of economic and socio-psychological methods. [211] Under socialism, "no conflict of interests between

---

[210] Lenin V.I. The State and Revolution. Collected works, 4th edition. V. 25. P. 445.

workers and employers can exist." [212] Rozmirovich used this contrived ideological concept to demonstrate that that any research into social problems of economic management was not needed.

Unfortunately, her passion for the technological approach entailed aggressive intolerance to any views other than her own. For instance, her voice stood out in the large chorus of critics who attacked Vitke's remarkable concept of management. Due to her efforts the discussion soon moved from science to politics, so Vitke had no chance whatsoever (we shall discuss it in greater detail in our next book). Rozmirovich in fact killed a promising trend in management theory using illegal weapons – that in a few years would be turned against herself...

(28) Lunacharsky, Anatoly Vasilyevich (1875 - 1933) - politician and statesman, writer, member of the USSR Academy of Sciences. People's Commissar of Education since 1917.

(29) Kuybyshev, Valerian Vladimirovich (1988 - 1935) - politician and statesman, Chairman of the Central Control Commission of the Party and simultaneously People's Commissar of RKI since 1923, Chairman of the Supreme Economic Council since 1926, chairman of Gosplan since 1930.

(30) Rubinshteyn, Modest Iosifovich (1894 - 1969) - economist, social activist, member of the Communist Academy, head of the science and technology policy department at Gosplan. In his works on economic development he focused on innovations in industry and management. He also advocated "the colossal advantages" of communist NOT over capitalist scientific management that ostensibly was hopelessly flawed and socially limited. See, for example, his "Capitalist innovations" (Moscow,

---

[211] Rozmirovich E. NOT, RKI and the Party. Moscow, 1926. P.198.
[212] Ibid.

1929) and "Science, technology and the economy in the Soviet Union and the capitalist countries" (Moscow- Leningrad, 1932)

(31) Noa, Fridrikh Georgievich in the 1920s was a well-known expert in the field of norms, standardization and improvements in labor and management, and a supporter of Gastev. Much like the director of TsIT, Noa believed that norms and standards catalyze productivity growth if they do not fossilize and turn into dogmas. See his "Issues of industrial innovation" (Moscow - Leningrad, 1924); "Government regulation of wages" (Moscow, 1928); "The problem of standardization in the USSR" ("Inzhenernyi trud", 1926, No. 3) and others.

(32) V.A. Nesmeyanov, a once well-known NOT scholar, is now all but forgotten. Let us try to fill this gap.

At the 1st NOT conference Nesmeyanov openly opposed major scholars of that time such as Academicians V.M. Bekhterev and O.A. Yermansky who rejected Taylorism as a system of utmost intensification of labor that ignored the findings of psychophysiology. Nesmeyanov argued there was a need to fight with the current routine system of management rather than with Taylorism that sought to destroy this system.[213]

Nesmeyanov defended the legitimacy of time studies that Yermansky, as we remember, spared neither time nor black inks to discredit. "Time studies are a means rather than the essence of the system."[214] He admitted Taylorism had its own imperfections but argued that, first, it was not the case with time studies and, second, one should "find ways to overcome" these flaws rather than engage in heavy rhetoric like Bekhterev and Yermansky. Nesmeyanov rightly pointed out that in an economy impoverished by the war and revolution the introduction of scientific management was difficult, yet badly needed. It was the only chance to efficiently use "the live workforce of the Republic" and prevent "mass extinction of the population." [215]

---

[213]Proceedings of the First All-Russian Initiating NOT Conference... Vol. 1. P. 77.
[214]Ibid. P. 76.

Nesmeyanov identified and articulated the difficulties that stood in the way of introducing scientific management in the harsh Russian reality.

First, Russian workers, technicians and even engineers know nothing about time and motion studies.

Second, the vast majority of workers and engineers firmly believe that Taylorism is "an anti-socialist sweatshop system ... that can only ruin workmen's health without any true results." Nesmeyanov notes that this conviction lingered because of "socialist parties, who vehemently opposed Taylorism in peacetime (remember Lenin's famous anti-Taylor articles of 1913) and continue their fight today... The current Conference is a striking example of this campaign. At this meeting a member of the party that opposes scientific management and an ardent personal enemy of this discipline for many years *(Yermansky, who at that time was still a member of the Menshevik party – author's note)* reverses his position and even moderates the panel on the practical application of NOT in Russia." [216] As a result, continued Nesmeyanov, in a devastated country, that has never seen any Taylorism and suffers a decline of industry, the first introduction to scientific management starts with preaching some safeguards against this system. "It's like as if a doctor prescribing an antipyretic and a palpitation remedy to a patient suffering from a weak heart and low body temperature. The outcome in this case would be a further weakening of NOT efforts and initiatives." We must admit that these observations sound highly relevant.

Third, the author notes, few managers wish to embrace scientific management. Some fear the new system would increase their workload, others just do not sympathize with the Bolshevik regime.

---

[215]Proceedings of the First All-Russian Initiating NOT Conference... Vol. 4. P. 43.
[216]Ibid. P. 44.

Fourth, there is a problem of material incentives, since monetary payments under the fixed wages system have little value, while a system of in-kind bonuses is ill-designed.

Fifth, numerous "special rations" received by engineers, executives and all kinds of bureaucrats in a non-transparent way "create reluctance to work in the masses and embitter them against the Soviet state."

Sixth, the lack of "tools, instruments and materials for scientific management such as stopwatches, forms, cards, often just a common watch." Speaking about this kind of difficulties Nesmeyanov referred to his own experience when he personally had to come up to the Chairman of the Supreme Economic Council, that was "no mean feat" in order just to "get a stopwatch", an absolute must for scientific management studies. But even after pleading with the highest authorities in government, the Party and trade unions, and using "whatever legal and illegal ways of speeding up business, I haven't been able to get the instruction on scientific output rate setting and time cards from the printer since last November," Nesmeyanov lamented. [217]

Thus, concluded Nesmeyanov, the implementation of scientific management in Russia calls for no less heroism and courage than the fronts of the Civil War.

How can these problems be solved or at least alleviated? Nesmeyanov came up with a number of practical suggestions. These include: training of time study instructors and development of time study guidelines; a broad Taylorism awareness campaign; introduction of scientific management courses at all educational establishments; a more careful selection of executives that would be loyal to the regime and, which is even more important, *would have their heart bleeding for Russia* and would be willing to help

---

[217]Ibid.

save it from economic collapse; abolition of restrictions on bonuses and the introduction of a *progressive remuneration system* that would in fact reduce costs due to increased efficiency; eradication of "special rations", "the evil of the Republic"; finally, government assistance to applied scientific management. [218]

It would be wrong, however, to assume that Nesmeyanov was just a practitioner without any talent for theory. He did formulate the fundamental principles of scientific management including:

1. Consistency of actions.
2. Division of labor.
3. Streamlined organization.
4. Proper accountability.
5. Encouraging grassroots innovation, initiative and linkage to progress.[219]

Consistency of actions implies unity of command in combination with collective consultations. The unity of command is necessary to ensure full responsibility for decisions and actions as well as their coordination. Collective consultations are needed to unlock the full potential of staff, enhance competence, fully assess the situation and occasionally correct the decision-maker.

Speaking of the division of labor, Nesmeyanov suggested a broad interpretation that includes not only the formal division of labor among team members (whose relevance is "no longer challenged by anyone,") but also that among management staff itself, an idea "that many people still do not appreciate". He believed that management should be divided into a variety of individual functions (design of tools, instruments and models; salary calculation; costing; control over materials; hiring; transportation;

---

[218]Ibid. P. 45-46.
[219]Nesmeyanov V.A. Factors and principles of enterprise management. [*O faktorakh i printcipakh organizatsii zavodoupravleniia*]. "Vremya", 1925, No. 9(21). P.17-18.

fixing output rates and so on) and also recommended that they be centralized.

Streamlined organization means a distinct division of functions among factory departments and a clear definition of authority, rights and duties of personnel in written job descriptions. Power and responsibility are inseparable, and so are rights and duties. Power without responsibility or responsibility without power are equally meaningless, he noted. Clear limits to power and responsibility may be established in practice only by a precise distribution of rights and duties.[220]

At this point Nesmeyanov recommends the following guidelines:

1. A manager burdened with too many duties will "discharge them poorly if at all."

2. Underusing a manager is equally bad for business (which hardly needs an explanation).

3. Each manager should be given as many duties as he can discharge at a high professional level. Every manager should deal directly with 4 or 5 subordinates.

We will not retell Nesmeyanov's ideas on materials control, initiative, grassroots innovation and linkage to progress. Let us just note that this author deserves to be returned from oblivion.

(33) Kan Iosif Abramovich (1884 - 1945) – an expert in innovation and production management who was well-known in his time. His works include, in particular, "The Socialist Industry" (Moscow, 1922); "American innovators. Essays and Studies" (Moscow-Leningrad, 1928, co-authored with Z.A. Paperny) and "Methods and techniques of innovation" ("Predpriyatie", 1927, No. 8).

---

[220]Ibid. P.20.

(34) Mikhailov Arseniy Vasilyevich, a TsIT fellow, was one of the most prominent Gastev's disciples and allies. His books include "The socialist organization of labor" (Moscow, 1927); " Taylor's System" (Leningrad, 1928); "Ford's System" (Moscow-Leningrad, 1928); "What is innovation in manufacturing" (Moscow, 1929)

(35) Vasiliev Mikhail Ilyich was a well-known NOT scholar and Gastev's supporter who is, unfortunately, completely forgotten nowadays. His numerous works include, among others, "Scientific organization of labor in the railway industry," (3rd ed., Petrograd, 1921), "Inspection and restructuring of enterprises and institutions," (Moscow, 1923) and "Raise the productivity of industry" (Leningrad, 1925). He had a number of interesting ideas pertaining to theory as well as practice. Let us dwell briefly on his views.

According to Vasiliev, the goal of any economic activity is to meet demand as fully as possible with the least means and effort, or, in other words, with the highest labor productivity. [221]

Productivity growth is an objective law applicable to all socio-economic formations. Two key factors increase productivity and advance the economy: the invention of better tools and implements, or improvement in the material factors of industry, and, secondly, better management and better use of workforce. Science can be a powerful catalyst of progress in both cases. On the other hand, while science and technology have been making an active and valuable contribution to the former area, until quite recently, i.e. before Taylor, it has "almost never ventured" into the latter field. Hence Vasiliev arrives at a fundamental conclusion that *a transition to a scientific management system is a historical necessity.* He believes that Taylor's discovery of scientific management "can easily compare with the greatest inventions that

---

[221]Vasiliev, M.I. Scientific management and the railway industry. [Nauchnaya organizatsiya truda i zheleznodorozhnoe khozyaystvo.] Third edition. Petrograd, , 1921. P. 6.

spelled revolution in their field."[222] As you can see, he unequivocally supports Taylorism.

Vasiliev clearly saw the challenges to scientific management practices. First of all, managers who are told that their ways are obsolete and they act more like "healers than professional doctors" feel that "their pride is insulted." He also identified other inhibiting factors such as the inertia of economic thinking and management stereotypes. The new system, he notes, necessitates dramatic changes in management style and methods. No wonder some people oppose the idea; moreover, not every manager is capable of accommodating new professional trends.

In his presentation at the 1st NOT conference Vasiliev expanded on this observation. Unfortunately, he said, most managers were still using routine attitudes such as "issuing circulars and requesting reports"[223] without caring for *the principle of profitability that results from prudent administration,* which still applies under socialism. Its essence, plain and simple, is that "Any enterprise in any situation must be sensibly organized so as to add value."

This principle, he continued, requires *substantial intensification of labor.* In heated discussions at the conference Vasiliev ardently defended the idea of time studies that was, as we remember, stigmatized by Russian "anti-Taylorists", particularly Bekhterev and Yermansky. "Time studies are a fundamental element of scientific management, - claimed Vasiliev, - no scientific management is conceivable without it." [224]

Vasiliev distinguished between two types of time studies. *The first one* "can be likened to taking a photograph that records events and things without any analysis." *The second one* is similar to a

---

[222]Ibid. P. 3.
[223]Proceedings of the First All-Russian Initiating NOT Conference... Vol. 3. P. 9.
[224]Ibid.

microscopic study of "constituent elements that build up the world: each of them is individually scrutinized, broken down into details, cleared of useless and harmful appendages to finally appear in a scientific and concentrated form." Unfortunately, he wrote, people often do not this difference; this may lead to confusion and even erroneous conclusions such as Yermansky's claim at the 1st conference that "time studies alone are good for nothing". They are not; Vasiliev proved their benefits by formulating clear guidelines for efficient time studies in the railway system.[225]

One of Vasiliev's achievements was an original *"clinical" method of scientific management.* Clinical diagnostics and treatment are a powerful instrument of progress in medicine, he wrote, "The economy, too, often needs a "clinical method" of systematic observation and measurement that is related to *scientific management"*[226] Moreover, the clinical method in fact *is* scientific management, Vasiliev claimed. The more cultured a patient is, the better he knows what to expect of the clinic and when he should schedule an appointment. As our industrial executives gain experience they knowledge, they will better realize what is to be expected from NOT, when a review is needed, and when their own ways and means or the "home first aid kit" would suffice.

Vasiliev's clinical method consists of a preliminary review of an enterprise, diagnostics and development of remedial measures. The review includes the following stages:

1. Setting objectives;
2. Selection and appointment of the reviewer;
3. Preliminary study of the enterprise;
4. Setting up a review team;
5. The main review process;

---

[225] Ibid. P. 110-111.
[226] Vasiliev M.I. On the use of NOT. *[O primenenii NOT]*. "Predpriyatie", 1924, No.1. P. 52.

6. Data analysis;

7. Drafting conclusions and recommendations;

8. Proposals on the implementation of recommendations and help in the organization of work. [227]

Vasiliev also had some other interesting ideas, including those related to theory and methodology.

(36) Andreev, Andrei Andreevich (1895 - 1971) - politician and statesman. Secretary of the CPSU (b) (1924-25). Chairman of the Central Control Commission, People's Commissar of RKI and Deputy Chairman of SNK (since 1930). People's Commissar of Railways (since 1931).

(37) Zinoviev, Grigory Yevseevich) (1883 – 1936) – a major politician, professional revolutionary, close friend of Lenin, member of the Politburo in 1921-1926. In 1934 he was arrested and sentenced to 10 years on false charges ("The Moscow Center" case); sentenced to death and executed in 1934. Exonerated posthumously in 1988.

(38) Tomsky, Mikhail Pavlovich (1880 – 1936) – a leading politician and statesman. Chairman of the All-Russian Central Council of Trade Unions for many years, member of the Central Committee of the Communist Party (1922-1930). A proponent of democracy in governance (which was rare for a Communist functionary), he always opposed the administrative command methods and bureaucracy in management. As early as in 1920, in the well-known discussion on trade unions, he firmly resisted the ideas of "revamping" trade-unions and converting them to "government proxies". At the 2nd NOT conference, as we have seen, Tomsky lent every bit of support to Gastev, a non-Communist, and protested against "partisan criticism" directed at Gastev by

---

[227] Vasiliev M.I. Process review and restructuring at enterprises and institutions. *[Obsledovanie i reorganizatsiya predpriyatiy i uchrezhdeniy.]* Moscow, 1923. P. 10-11.

Kerzhentsev and other supporters of the "Communist" NOT. No need to say this support was invaluable. In the late 1920s Tomsky openly challenged the despotic methods of governance practiced by Stalin and his henchmen, including the "extraordinary measures" involved in collectivization and industrialization. His position was branded "the right-wing deviation" in the Party. Later, as mass purges were on the rise, Tomsky committed suicide. He was posthumously exonerated.

(39) Shmidt, Vasiliy Vasilievich (1886 – 1938) – a communist party functionary and a statesman. People's Commissar of Labor (1918-1928). An avid supporter of Gastev and his institute. Executed and posthumously exonerated.

(40) Dunaevsky, Fedor Romanovich (1887 - 1960) – a world-renowned scientific management scholar, professor, founder and director of the Ukrainian Institute of Labor (Kharkov), that was rated abroad at par with the best research centers in Western Europe.[228]

Dunaevsky's theories rely on his *firm belief that organization plays a key role in society and in the economy.* He maintained that a healthy national economy and robust growth absolutely require a smooth and synchronized operation of the sophisticated system of management.

He observed that the current management system fell short of supporting a dynamic economy. This misaligned system lacked internal harmony and thus regularly stalled. A sound management system, on the contrary, *must be an integrated structure whose elements are interconnected, "a holistic complex" rather than "a bunch of isolated actions."*[229] The lack of such a complex system, Dunaevsky surmised, was not merely a theoretical issue. Whenever the principle of integration is ignored, errors, omissions and other unpleasant surprises are in stock for the practical manager.

---

[228] See "Sistema i organizatsiya", 1925, No. 12. P. 81.
[229] Dunaevsky F.R. Comprehensive organization. *[Kompleksnost v organizatsii.]* "Trudy Vseukrainskogo instituta truda", issue 2, Kharkov. 1928. P.4.

Dunaevsky concluded that the approach to scientific management can be "fragmented" as opposed to "integrated" (or comprehensive). Using a metaphor, he explained that the difference between the two was "about the same as that between an ignorant fanatic who declares that a certain medicine is a universal remedy, and a professional doctor who issues prescriptions based on a comprehensive exam and all the particular features of the case."[230] Dunaevsky, therefore, came up with a *key idea of a comprehensive approach to scientific management issues.*

Dunaevsky's numerous works contain many more exciting ideas and concepts that were substantially ahead of their time. Considering, however, that a separate treatise on this scholar will be published under this project, let us not go too fast right now.

(41) Unfortunately, what materialized was the grim part of Gastev's forecast: the Taganrog Institute of scientific organization of labor and production lost all financial and logistical support from the government and had to close down in the late 1920s.

---

[230] The position of Kharkov Labor Institute on the Organization of Labor. *[Pozitsiya Kharkovskogo instituta truda otnositelno organizatsii truda.]* "Trudy Vseukrainskogo instituta truda", issue 1, Kharkov. 1923. P.3.